To Steph.

Real Life
DRESSAGE

enjoy the Read!

Best wishes Carl Hester x.

Real Life
DRESSAGE

Training Advice from Novice to Grand Prix

CARL HESTER and Polly Ellison

KENILWORTH PRESS

First published in 2004 by
Kenilworth Press Ltd
Addington
Buckingham MK18 2JR

Reprinted 2004

British Library Cataloguing in Publication Data
A catalogue record for this book is available from the
British Library

ISBN 1-872119-49-2

Design by Paul Saunders
Layout by Kenilworth Press
Printed and bound in Malta on behalf of Compass Press Ltd

Frontispiece photo on page 2:
Carl and Donner Rhapsody (Madonna).

Contents

Photo credits

All photos are by **Trevor Meeks**, with the exception of the following:

David Charles – pages 2, 8, 24, 81, 93 and 95

Kevin Sparrow – page 28

Polly Ellison – pages 103, 111, 115, 116 and 117

Acknowledgements

Training horses from youngsters to Grand Prix, and winning at all levels on the way, is very much a team effort. In the same way so was the writing of this book. We would like to thank everyone at Hooze Farm for their assistance, especially Kate and Stuart Carter whose beautiful home it is, and our thanks too to all the team who work there. Photo and special training sessions can be disruptive, so their patience and goodwill was much appreciated.

We would especially like to thank Spencer Wilton, who did such an excellent job of riding for the photo-shoot, enabling Carl to oversee from the ground. As a top rider in his own right we were grateful for Spencer's expertise, which brought out the best in every horse. Spencer was also instrumental in gathering everyone together to contribute their respective parts to the book, which again was incredibly helpful.

Also, our special thanks go to Carl's brilliant groom, Caroline Dawson, who saw that all the horses arrived for the photos looking fantastic. Her dedication to these horses on a day-to-day basis plays an important part in the success of the team. Likewise, grateful thanks to vet Buffy Shirley-Beavan and physiotherapist Maggie Turner for giving up their time to tell us more about their work, which underlined the importance of their contribution to the team.

Photographer Trevor Meeks deserves a mention here for his superb pictures which illustrate the book.

We would like to thank the owners for letting us use their horses as examples – especially when we have to mention the horses' weaknesses as well as their strengths in order to illustrate the work that is required to overcome certain problems. As we mention in the book, all the horses have great potential, which is so exciting, but it is also important to remember that there is no such thing as the perfect dressage horse!

Finally, Polly would like to give special thanks to Rob Adams for looking after a herd of badly behaved would-be dressage horses, and to Belinda Ellison for caring for a group of naughty cats while the book was being written.

CARL HESTER AND POLLY ELLISON

Introduction

It may surprise you to discover that all the horses introduced in this book are horses who have problems. None of them is perfect – because in real life dressage the perfect horse doesn't exist. The aim of my book is not to describe ideal training scenarios but to look at what we can do, to the best of our ability, with the horses we have. Difficult horses can become good horses, as I have proved with Escapado; and it is important not to give up until you are absolutely sure it's not going to work. If there is a glimmer of hope, it is worth persevering. It might take longer to get there, but if you, the rider, have the patience it may well still be possible - and this is just as true at the higher levels as it is at the lower ones.

The Horses

All the horses featured in this book have Grand Prix as a goal. In fact, I would not be working with them if I thought they were not going to make it. While it is possible that not all of them will reach such dizzy heights, there is a good chance that one or two will. The interesting thing about these horses is that they are a cross-section of different personalities and different types; some big movers, some not so big; some energetic, some lazy – but as I discuss how I train each one with Grand Prix as the ultimate goal, I hope to show you how different methods apply to different horses.

FACING PAGE: Carl and Donnersong celebrate together.

SUPERMAN

5 years old
Bay gelding standing 15.3 hands high
By Metal out of a Voltaire mare
Owned by: Charlotte Hughes
Wins include:
- Equilibra Champion 2003

This neat, compact little horse is strong in his body, particularly for a horse of his age. His legs are perhaps a little short for a horse of his length and depth. Despite his tender years, he is already capable of very powerful movement, despite the fact that he has barely started any form of training regime.

He has an intelligent head, small pretty ears with a good-shaped mouth that fits the bit very easily. (It is important that the tongue groove is wide enough to allow the tongue to lie comfortably and not be pushed upwards.) His tongue is not too big, which is important, especially in dressage, as there needs to be room for the snaffle bit and ultimately the double bridle.

Superman has an attractive head and his sensible, kind expression reflects his willing, workmanlike approach to his training. The head and overall expression can tell a potential buyer a great deal about a horse.

There is plenty of room in his neck for the flexion that is required to enable him to be ridden on the bit when asked.

Markings play an important part in a horse's overall expression. In Superman's case he has a very attractive star, perfectly positioned on his forehead, which gives the impression of broadening the forehead.

Tip

It is important to see that there is space for at least two fingers directly behind the cheek bone, and that the cheek bone is not too large. If a large cheek bone is combined with a thick neck, it tends to create a bulge of fatty tissue where the space should be. This would result in the horse finding flexion difficult, if not impossible. All in all, the point where the neck meets the head should not be too thick nor too thin; the set and connection of the head and neck are so important in the dressage horse.

Finally, he is slightly higher in the croup than at the withers which, had he not been a young horse may have been a problem, but I would expect a five-year-old to change shape, and certainly his fantastic movement far outweighs his conformation faults at present.

I would describe Superman as a natural athlete who, as he gets stronger becomes more opinionated, but is still a very willing worker.

PRO SET

7 years old
Bay stallion standing 16.1 hands high
By Jet Set out of a Flemmingh mare
Owned by: Meadow Stud
Wins include:

- Runner-up Novice Championships 2002
- In the top three in Shearwater Championships 2003
- Runner-up Medium Championships Winter 2004

Pro Set is a young stallion. These photos were taken during the breeding season, so he is not particularly well covered, which is often the case when a stallion is working and serving mares.

Pro has a fantastic top line, which is passed on to all his stock, together with a beautiful head and long neck. His length of neck enhances his appearance when he is on the bit, as he is open in the front and finds it easier to bend in comparison to

Tip

Care of the back is of primary importance with all breeding stallions. It is important that they do not develop weaknesses in this area.

Tip

Mouth size needs to be considered when choosing a potential dressage horse. If the size of the tongue is a problem it cannot be rectified by endeavouring to close the mouth up, or some such similar measure, as this only serves to increase the discomfort for the horse and therefore the problems.

a horse with a short, muscular neck.

Currently he is significantly stronger in the front than he is behind, with good muscles on the shoulder. The hindquarters will become stronger with work, particularly over the winter, with careful, correct training, and his training regime will take into account the fact that he is not yet a mature horse.

Pro has good sloping pasterns, which make him a comfortable ride. This is an important aspect since a short, upright pastern will not be as comfortable as far as riding is concerned. However, pasterns which are too long can be weak and liable to strain.

Pro's head is extremely attractive and he has the alert expression I would hope to see in a stallion. He has good, wide nostrils and pretty little ears, with a lovely big eye and good markings. These aspects, combined with the wonderful way he carries his neck, make him show-horse quality and portray him as the very kind stallion that he is.

I would describe Pro as a 'hot' type of horse who is very intelligent and quick to learn, but who just needs to gain confidence and strength before I can ask for more collection.

GROOVE JET

Stable name : Hector
8 years old
Bay gelding standing 17.2 hands high
By Jet Set out of a Clavicimbel mare
Owned by: Kenny Earle and Carl Hester
Wins include:

- Novice Champion 2002
- 3rd Shearwater Championships 2003
- Medium Winter Championships winner 2004

Hector's personality is really very endearing. He is a wonderfully kind and lovable character, which rather goes against the grain for horses with too much white in their eye (which he has). Superstition has it that horses with this trait are untrustworthy, and this could not be further from the truth with Hector. Possibly he is an exception to the rule, so it is a good idea to take note of a horse's eye and its general alertness. Large eyes, set well apart, are said to denote intelligence and generosity, while a dull eye combined with unpricked ears may be a sign of a lethargic or unhealthy horse. Hector's white eye has been passed down from his dam's sire, Clavicimbel, who became a Grand Prix horse at seven, so on this basis the white eye theory is disproved. Although Hector's eye is slightly on the small side, he still has a good neck and expressive face, especially when his ears are pricked.

From the point of view of his conformation, he is a very big gangly horse that needs to strengthen up. At his age he is not conditioned as his muscles are not developed, so his hind legs do not look quite as strong as those of some other horses of a comparable age. His neck needs more muscle on the top, and although he does not have a badly shaped neck, it does come out of the shoulder slightly lower than ideally I would like. This factor, combined with his size, which at eight years old is over 17.2 hh, has made it difficult to get him up off the forehand, but his very good hind-leg action, together with his movement, has helped create some good suspension. Once he is muscled up on his big frame his conformation will improve dramatically and he will be a very good stamp of horse.

Hector is a much 'slower' horse than Pro, and while no longer lazy he could have been described as such when he was four and five years old. Now he is older, he is a much hotter horse, which is either the result of the way I have trained him or simply that as a big horse, it has taken him time to find his strength and balance. Now he has achieved this he finds going forward much easier.

Tip

When a hind leg is well placed an imaginary vertical line should be traceable from the point of the buttock, down the back of the hock, then continuing down the back of the hind leg to the fetlock. The stifle joint should be close to the body but turned slightly outwards to enable free movement. The hock should be wide when seen from the side, and thick when seen from the rear, and its overall appearance should be one of bony strength. This area of conformation is all important as, after all, it is the powerhouse of the horse!

DOLENDO

Stable name: Donald

10 years old

Chestnut gelding standing 17.3 hands high

By Donnerhall out of a Pik Ramiro mare

Owned by: Ann Cory and Carl Hester

Wins include:

- Badminton Young Dressage Horse Championship
- Elementary Winter Championship Champion
- Medium Champion 2001
- Medium and Advanced Medium National Champion 2002
- Intermediaire I Champion 2003
- First International was a win

Donald has a very intelligent head with very good openness in his jaw line. He has good markings, and his white blaze giving the appearance of being completely level as he comes towards you. Asymmetrical stripes or blazes can be a disadvantage because they can make a horse look like it is head-tipping (when in fact it is not) or can emphasise an existing head-tip.

His eyes show intelligence and they are well set apart; his overall appearance being one of interest, calmness and friendliness.

One thing that does stand out about Donald's conformation is that he has a fabulous neck for dressage. It is round, uphill and very well set on, with a very strong shoulder to complete a very attractive picture. One disadvantage he has,

though, is that he is slightly croup-high, and as a result it has taken time to develop strength in his back. However, he is a strong type of horse who was initially, when younger, much bigger in front than behind. By the time he was nine his back end caught up with his very strong front end, which enhanced his good sloping quarters and his very strong hocks. This area is important because as a horse advances in training, more weight is transferred onto the hindquarters, hocks and hind legs, so a horse that does not have good conformation in this area will be at a severe disadvantage when its training gets to a more advanced level.

As with Pro, Donald has good sloping pasterns, making him a very comfortable ride. This is because the joints are lower to the floor, so the horse moves more softly. This is in contrast to more upright pasterns, which tend to send more concussion up through the leg to the shoulder, so making the ride less comfortable.

Although Donald is a big horse who has taken time to develop, he has now muscled up well, and has all the presence, looseness and stature of a true Grand Prix horse. As a youngster he was extremely naughty, being lazy and nappy, yet at the same time a really loving horse in the stable. It was his kind, affectionate way that kept us all going, as in the early days he clearly had an aversion to being ridden! Six years down the line he has settled down and is full of presence and, although still a little tense in the ring, is going in the right direction.

ESCAPADO

Stable name: Peanuts
11 years old
Bay gelding standing 16.2 hands high
By Ex Libris out of an Ikarus mare
Owned by: Roly Louard and Carl Hester
Wins include:

- Advanced Medium Champion 2001
- PSG and Intermediaire Champion 2002
- Runner-up in Grand Prix National Championships 2003
- Won and placed internationally, including Lipica and Spain 2004
- Selected for Athens Olympics 2004

Peanuts has a strong top line with high positioning of his head. In his case this is not a fault, but it could have been if it had come out of a straight shoulder, or if he had had a large muscle underneath his neck.

He has a good, sloping shoulder from his wither to the point of his shoulder. As a result the saddle sits well behind the shoulder, which means the weight of the rider is in a better place for the horse's balance. His wither is higher than his croup, and he has a fairly short, strong back which is workmanlike. He also has a very good hock action - his hocks step under the middle of his stomach with relative ease.

The line from elbow to stifle is very good and it gives him the impression of being built uphill. His tail is well set on, not too low and, as with Donald, Peanuts too has a good line from buttock to hock, and down to the fetlock. He has good hocks for dressage, being strong and able to take the weight for the more advanced movements.

He is blessed with good feet too, which is essential as most lameness comes from the feet. In the photo here he shows excellent condition and his well-developed muscles show him to be in perfect condition for Grand Prix work.

His expression is one of alertness, with relatively small ears and a generous eye. His length of mouth indicates that he can take the bit easily, and he has plenty of space behind the cheek bones, which allows him to flex correctly. The 'U' shape of his gullet allows plenty of openness and ease for breathing.

He is a 'hot' type, in fact the hottest of them all, but he has always been willing to work, and really the hotness made him try too hard when it came to it. He has always had a natural flight instinct, which makes him tense and try to run away from his problems. Now he is at Grand Prix level the best thing is that he is settled in his work and able to turn his negative tension into positive energy.

Chapter One

Training Principles

The aim of this book is to explain in simple terms the training methods I use with my horses. The book elaborates on some of the advice in my previous book, *Down to Earth Dressage*, and goes further, carrying on where that book left off.

I will describe the dressage movements involved, following some of my own horses up the levels to Grand Prix, examining the problems that are common to those movements, and looking at how I and other riders might overcome them. I have deliberately chosen horses with differing conformations and mental attitudes in order to illustrate the factors that need to be taken into account when training a horse to these levels.

As you will see, my own training philosophy is very much on the lines of the German training system, the *Richtlinien* or broad path, that the German trainers use so successfully. It allows for some personal interpretation of the 'scales of training' while setting parameters or ground rules which should be adhered to. I am therefore beginning the book with a reminder of the scales of training, which form the basis for all horses as they set out on their competition careers, whatever the discipline they may compete in eventually. The scales of training should act as your checklist – something that you are able to measure your horse's basic training against before you attempt to move up the levels. If you feel that your horse is working well within these guidelines then it is possible to move confidently forward to the higher levels in dressage. The scales of training provide a systematic physical and gymnastic education aimed at developing a horse's natural physical and mental aptitude to the full as well as establishing obedience.

Let's move on to the 'technical bit'.

The Scales of Training

The scales of training essentially consist of three phases, which are then broken down into six sections which all blend into each other. The time spent in each section depends on each individual horse but the aim is to ensure they are all sufficiently supple and 'through' at all times.

In the first of the phases, which looks at the initial ridden training of a young horse, the following are essential:

- **Rhythm**

- **Suppleness and Looseness**

- **Contact (acceptance of the bit)**

With these three areas to focus on, a rider takes the horse through an acclimatisation or familiarisation phase, which forms the foundation of the horse's training for the future.

With the first phase established, the rider can move on to the second phase, which looks at the development of pushing power or forward thrust. This includes all of the above and introduces:

- **Impulsion and Straightness**

The final phase is about the development of carrying capacity which, when all the other factors come together, should enable the horse to reach its ultimate goal:

- **Collection**

The combination of all these elements produces:

- **'Throughness'**

known in German as *Durchlassigkeit*.

Not only does this system provide a solid platform for young horses but it also offers a foundation for more advanced horses to adhere to, in a condensed form, in each lesson. In addition, it can form a base to which a horse can return to find security and relaxation if a more advanced lesson has caused tension or stress. It certainly works for my horses.

Riders should constantly remind themselves of these principles, not just in the early stages of training, but as they progress up the levels. Only when all these elements come together can a correct end result be achieved.

Let's now look at each of these elements in closer detail.

Rhythm

Rhythm is important. Horses with rhythm have regular steps or strides in each gait, the steps covering the same distance for the same duration. Rhythm should be maintained through transitions and turns, as well as on straight lines. For example, in the trot each diagonal should cover the same amount of ground and the beat should be regular. The training is incorrect if there is a loss of rhythm.

Suppleness and Looseness

This is an essential quality in early training. A horse must be working through its back with its muscles free of tension. It must be physically and mentally free from tension so it can use itself to the full. Joints should bend and straighten equally on each side of its body, and the horse must be attentive to its work. Signs that a horse is loose and relaxed are when it has a contented expression (through ears and eyes), its back swings rhythmically, its mouth is closed (but not immobile), and its tail is carried and swings in time to the movement. 'Snorting' also indicates that a horse is mentally relaxed. When a horse stretches its head and neck forward and downwards in all three gaits then looseness has been achieved.

Contact

By contact is meant a soft, steady connection between the rider's hand and the horse's mouth. The horse should go forward from the rider's driving aids and 'seek' a contact with the rider's hand. A correct, steady contact allows the horse to find its balance under the rider and a rhythm in each of the gaits. It should

A novice horse, slightly long but round in his frame. From a training point of view this is what a rider would want to achieve on a daily basis with a horse at this level.

never be achieved by a backward action of the hands but through the correctly delivered forward thrust of the hind legs. The horse goes forward confidently as a result of the rider's driving aids.

Impulsion

This is when the energy created by the hind legs is being transmitted into the gait and all aspects of the forward movement. The horse should push off energetically from the ground and swing its feet well forward. To work with impulsion in trot and canter the horse must have looseness with a springy, swinging back and a soft, correct contact. Good impulsion occurs when the hocks are carried energetically forwards and upwards immediately after the feet leave the ground. The horse's back muscles absorb the movement so the rider can sit softly and 'go with' the movement. Impulsion is created by training as the rider uses the horse's natural paces, but in addition ensures looseness, forward thrust and suppleness.

Once the contact has been established, the novice horse can progress to being ridden up more. However, daily work should be carried out in working mode to establish rhythm and balance with the more extravagant work saved for competitions.

Straightness

A horse is straight when its forehand is in line with its hindquarters. Straightness ensures that the weight is evenly distributed over the two halves of the body (so saving wear and tear) and is developed through systematic training and suppling of both sides of the body equally.

Most horses are naturally crooked, and the fact that the shoulders are narrower than the hindquarters results in further crookedness. If truly straight, the horse can use both hind legs equally and effectively, it can stay on the aids properly and develop suppleness, and it can have an even contact on both sides – and so can obtain collection. Only when straight can a horse be equally supple and 'through' on both reins.

Straightening a horse is an on-going process; without continual attention and work on this aspect of training the horse will revert to its natural crookedness.

Collection

A horse's weight, plus that of its rider, must be as evenly distributed as possible over all four legs. This means transferring the weight off the forelegs, which naturally carry more load than the hind legs, and increasing the weight on the hind legs, which were mainly intended to create forward movement. In collection the hind legs bend more, stepping further underneath the horse in

The ultimate in collection is the piaffe. Although in the early stages of his career, Escapado demonstrates the ability to carry the weight on his hind legs in piaffe.

the direction of the centre of gravity and so taking a greater share of the load. This lightens the forehand, giving more freedom of movement to the forelegs so the horse looks and feels more 'uphill'. The steps are shorter but do not lose energy or activity and so become more expressive. By training and developing the right muscles, the hindquarters can carry more, and increased flexion of the hind legs results in the neck being raised. When sufficiently developed, the horse can move in balance and self-carriage in all three gaits.

'Throughness' (Durchlassigkeit)

Finally, 'throughness', which means that a horse is prepared to accept the rider's aids willingly and without tension. It should respond obediently and equally on both reins, to driving, restraining and sideways-acting aids, showing it is a correctly schooled horse.

With each of my horses, no matter what type or temperament, the fundamental ground rules from the scales of training apply. In working up the levels to Grand Prix you will see that I regularly refer back to various aspects of the training scale, as I believe these ground rules should be applied constantly if you want to get the best out of your horses.

Donald exhibiting 'throughness' in his work.

Chapter Two

Top Dressage Horses
– Are They Born or Made?

Top dressage horses come in a variety of shapes and sizes. The purpose of this book is to help you with your training, whatever your horse's shape or size, since the success of any horse is dependent on a rider's full understanding of his horse and its particular needs, combined, of course, with the horse's willingness to work.

Before looking at the training itself I'd like to talk about some elements that should be considered when looking for a good dressage horse.

What Do You Look for in a Dressage Horse?

When asked this question, most people say: 'the trot!' It is generally thought that the bigger the horse's trot, the better it will be at dressage. However, a big-moving horse can have its own problems. Although there are aspects of the trot which are important, it is vital to remember that what a rider should be looking for first is the right type of horse. Huge movers can find the work extremely difficult, and although they have potential, riders must not underestimate the problems that they can encounter when buying an extravagant-moving horse. For example, a big-moving horse does not necessarily always have the speed in the hind legs, which develop collection, nor is it able to attain the degree of flexion required for piaffe. It is also important to remember that you can change a horse's trot, but, as this book will illustrate later on, the walk and the canter are much harder to influence.

What is a Good Temperament?

I put horses into two main categories: 'The Whoa' and 'The Go'. All riders are different: some don't like hot horses, preferring instead to push their horses, while others like to hang on. It is possible that lazy horses can make Grand Prix horses just as easily as the hotter types. The lazier types might need only twenty minutes to work in, but then a horse does not have to be worked for one and a

Escapado showing submissive concentration.

half hours to prove it is a Grand Prix prospect. In the case of slower horses you have to learn how to work them. If they are more phlegmatic they usually do not have to do their movements all the time; sometimes it is simply a matter of a quick suppling and then they just go out and do it.

What is important is that the horse really wants to do the job and is happy to work with **you**, the rider.

Looks versus 'Feel'

Strange as it may sound, do not always be put off by what you see. Sometimes it does not matter if a young horse does not move brilliantly. If possible, get on and 'feel' it. Some horses that do not look as though they have the biggest movement are totally different when you sit on them. It is not impossible to discover that not only do they have movement when sat on but also, and more importantly, they have rhythm, which as a rider you know you can do something with. Rhythm is so important.

I have a useful test that gives me an 'indication' of what the horse's ability may be in the future. This is something I do regularly at home with our youngsters, and it can easily be carried out when looking to buy a horse. Each horse reacts differently, and it is simply a question of testing the horse's reactions to the touch (and I mean 'touch') of a whip on the hindquarters. For example, if you do this with Superman he automatically sinks his bottom down and gets agitated. This tells me that one day, with this sort of reaction, he will be easy to teach the advanced movements to because he is very sharp, quick and his natural reaction is to lower himself and bring his hind legs underneath him. Pro Set reacts in a similar fashion to Superman, although he is not so underneath himself naturally (but that is simply because at present he lacks strength). I know that with correct training he will do it easily enough. Groove

Pro Set giving his rider an amazing feeling in his extended trot, which achieves top marks.

Superman showing the true three-beat required in the canter.

Jet, on the other hand, did not react to the whip because he was too big and too slow. However, as his training progresses he is becoming sharper and with the correct exercises and getting him 'off the leg' he is now showing great promise. Dolendo was a similar horse to Groove Jet and learned in the same way, by doing the correct exercises – although it has to be said that we never touched him with a whip because he was so naughty.

This simple exercise, which should never be done in a threatening way, does reveal a great deal to the rider about that particular horse.

Assessing Rideability

This is something that you will definitely need your future dressage horse to possess. The horse has got to want to work, so willingness plays a very big part in rideability. I'm talking here about the horse's desire to go forward, to work with the rider not against him, as well as having the ability to 'go off the leg' so that he (the horse) can collect or lengthen with suppleness and energy. When trying a horse I always ask myself: 'Does this horse allow itself to be ridden in a supple way?' A horse that is holding itself against the rider is not evincing rideability, whereas one that lets go, bends and is supple is showing rideability.

Superman's rideability always stood out. Currently he would rate 10 out of 10. For his age he is amazingly supple, forward and balanced and he will do whatever I, as his rider, ask. He is naturally gifted, but does not possess perfect conformation – his neck is not ideal as it lacks length. However, he has a mouth that is so soft, and he is so completely relaxed on the bit through the jaw that it would be correct to say that he is naturally 'built on the bit'.

It is important when assessing rideability to take shape and size into account. A small, compact horse (like Superman) could find the early work easier than a big horse (like Groove Jet). Groove Jet, as a four-year-old, did not want to work, not because he was against the rider but simply because he was not strong enough. He knew his limitations.

Many different types of horse make it to Grand Prix. Compare Gigolo, Bonfire, Granat and Rembrandt, for example. These four horses had less-than-perfect conformation and, looks-wise, ranged from beauty to beast, yet they all made Grand Prix very successfully.

> **Reaching the top** has more do with rideability and movement, and less to do with make and shape.

Movement Through Rideability

Movement can be created through rideability. The key is knowing when to create that extra movement and when to save the horse. This is paramount to the welfare of the horse as it starts its training up the levels. For example, there is a 'show trot' and a 'training trot'. The latter should be easy and not put any strain or pressure on the joints. The show trot, however, is big and powerful, and is achieved through careful training, taking time to develop the necessary suppleness in the joints to sustain such movement without jarring or straining. The training should be such that the horse can turn the show trot on when you need it. This comes about only when sufficient strength has been built up. It should not be attempted until you arc confident that the strength is there. This highlights a problem with the bigger-moving horses as you have to question whether or not a big-moving four-year-old's joints will stand up to the work ahead, to enable it to still be competing at eighteen years old. If you buy a good walk and a good canter, you can develop the trot if it's not special at this age.

Another aspect of this is if a horse has a particular talent for something. If this is the case it is important not to overwork the talent but to save it for show days. Corlandus, ridden by Margit Otto-Crepin for France, was a perfect example of this. The horse was gifted with one of the best piaffes and passages of his day, so his rider would save these movements for the shows. This meant that the horse really wanted to perform them when asked, keeping the work fresh and exciting to watch.

I believe that riders should avoid repeatedly doing their favourite exercises, or those of their horses, and should, instead, focus on their problem areas. They should stick to the essentials that make for the best training and preparation for competition. However, it does not mean that at the end of the training session, they cannot finish off with one or two easier or special exercises, thus ending on a good note.

Donnersong on his victory lap after winning the Hartpury Derby. This photo shows how flexible the joints have to be. Note the inside hind fetlock and the degree of flexion whilst he is doing his special canter.

Intelligent Horses Need Intelligent Riders

Make no mistake, talented horses are very intelligent. All my top horses have been clever individuals. Smart, inquisitive youngsters need discipline but their questioning of things at shows, for example, should be tolerated to a certain extent. Working a horse up the levels helps a rider understand his horse, but it is important that a rider does not lose patience and takes time to understand. The majority of horses take time to mature both physically and mentally and it is very important to remember this.

Chapter Three

Intelligent Riding

Training Regimes

Normally, all our horses have a seven-day working week. They school on a Monday and Tuesday, then hack or lunge on Wednesday, then school again on Thursday and Friday. They are lunged, hacked or perhaps just get turned out on Saturday; and all the horses go hacking on Sundays when the roads are quiet and therefore safer.

When summer comes, and there are more shows to attend, then this obviously changes somewhat, but they would always be schooled or trained before a show, and in the lead-up to a show, more work gets done. We don't just concentrate on doing softening, elastic exercises but instead do more on school movements, stringing some of the movements together, and maybe even practise riding a test. However, in winter we don't do any test riding. Winter is all about bending, stretching and teaching new things as the horses become stronger.

The day after a show the horses tend either to be ridden out in walk on a hack or to be turned out. I do not believe in horses standing in their stables for a day off. All my horses get out every day, one way or another, whether it means going for a hack, or going into the pen or into the field. Hacking is very important, not just to let horses unwind, but because it gets them used to 'hazards', such as dustbins and other people's dogs, and they meet other horses when out hacking, which is all good experience for them.

Warming Up and Cooling Down

It is very important to a horse's well-being that these two areas of work are incorporated into the daily training programme. At home we are lucky in that we can warm up by spending fifteen minutes walking around a farm track before schooling begins. The horses are all walked on a long rein, stretching their necks out, while warming up their muscles in a relaxed way, culminating in a walk up a hill

Escapado working on flexion and submission during the warming-up phase.

before going into the indoor school to start work. Once in the school the horses stretch and work on transitions, such as trot to canter, canter to trot, gradually making the work more demanding but ensuring that the obedience and the 'swing' is established first. The work at the beginning is all about stretching, not carrying. It changes to carrying power when we move on to the more collected work, which involves getting the horse to engage its hind legs more. Once the collected work is over, the horse then goes back to stretching down again, so relaxing the muscles and finally finishing with a walk around the field to unwind mentally.

There are days, especially with the more tense horses such as Escapado, when the rider should not do anything other than stretching, because this keeps the horse's mind relaxed. For a lazier type of horse, too much stretching can make them too relaxed and they can end up towing around the school on their head. These horses need to do more work up on the bit in their sessions, so that they are kept sharper, and they should be kept more engaged by plentiful transitions. Hotter types that are trying too hard need to spend more of their session with their neck down and at full stretch. There is no reason why they cannot do the movements in the stretch position. A rider can still do a half-pass with his horse's neck stretched. The same applies to canter pirouettes. They do not always have to be up on the bit.

The key is to know your horse and its personality and then design a routine according to its needs. Also you need to take into account the natural elements:

for example, if it is windy, hot or very wet. When ridden in the rain, Escapado always runs around so that he does not get wet. He likes to spend time in the field, and has problems when he can't be turned out because, say, the ground is waterlogged. Over a period of time you will discover your horse's personality and can adopt a routine to suit him.

Bear in mind the age of the horse, too. Four- and five-year-olds are immature, and do not know their own strength when it comes to disagreements; but by the time they get to five and six they become more opinionated and strong. They are also growing up in front one moment, and up behind the next. All this must be taken into account when planning a routine for the horse.

Repetition

Be aware of your horse and have the patience to wait for your hard work to be rewarded. I will never say that a horse will not do something, because I now know that many horses can change as they find their balance and become submissive. Work through your problems, and once you understand your horse then the key is repetition. This is how the horse learns, and it comes through having a structured way of working and riding. For example, if a horse pulls on the right, the rider must ask why? It may well be because the horse is stiff on the right, so you have to repeat the suppling exercises until your horse learns to be more supple on that side. You cannot expect the horse to do an exercise once and then assume it knows what to do. You must repeat it until the horse is strong enough and supple enough to learn to carry itself straight.

Movements that always need perfecting are square halts, rein backs and walk pirouettes, and riders must put in the time to get these right. If you cannot canter up the centre line and make a perfect halt, it will be judged, purely and simply, as rider error. It is a question of discipline and there is no excuse for not getting an eight for your centre line.

In fact, you can take time to practise halting to give your horse a break in his work. You might be lucky enough to have someone on the ground or a mirror to hand, otherwise you just have to check yourself. Whatever the circumstances, establishing square halts at every opportunity is good for young horses and doesn't wear them out. Superman does not naturally have a square halt yet, but this is something that will come with time.

Signs of Tension

As a rider you must be able to feel how your horse is in your hand. Has he become strong? Has he become one-sided? These are signs that tension is creeping in. Listen, too, to the horse's breathing. When Escapado is nervous or stressed, he always starts to breathe heavily. Other indicators of tension are a lack of response to the leg, when the horse pushes his body against the rider, or flightiness, with the horse uncharacteristically running away from the leg.

Dolendo showing a four-square halt, achieved after many hours of practice.

Remember it is always possible to take a horse to a show just to get him used to the atmosphere, work him until he is relaxed, then to put him back on the lorry and take him home. That way he has learned a great deal and you can enjoy your horse.

Listen to your horse and you will begin to identify potential problems.

The key to overcoming tension lies in relaxation, and this will depend on each individual horse, again underlying the necessity for getting to know your horse. Take Escapado, for example: when he gets into a stressful situation, for instance when he is learning something new, like one-time changes all the way round a circle, then his breathing gets very noisy and he gets tense. I then start to talk to him and as a result his breathing quietens down until I cannot hear it.

It is so important to listen. The more you observe about the horse you are riding, the more likely you are to know when to do the most appropriate exercise for that horse so that you do not create a problem but actually overcome one.

Routine

Routine is important, especially for young horses. Having a set routine, and working at a slightly higher level than you would compete the horse, enables the rider to cope when out competing, where the distractions are so much greater. The distractions make the horse stiff and tense, so to be trying to work on more difficult, less established exercises at shows results in the rider struggling to get the horse's attention, whereas a routine where the exercises are well known reassures the horse and limits the problems the rider encounters.

Know Your Horse, and Adapt the Training

It is not possible to make a dressage horse simply by schooling it harder and harder. If a horse has natural ability but comes up against a mental or physical problem then it is worth persevering. When a rider encounters problems, sometimes the solution lies in looking at alternative ways to achieve the same end. In the case of Donald, whom I rode to medium, it became apparent that he would need more time than I could give him, so Spencer took over the ride, as he was able to give him this time, and as a result has made a real partnership with him.

Peanuts is a full-time job. I have had to create a special training structure for him, for when he attends competitions. At shows I have to spend time hacking him, letting him graze and generally winning his trust. I ride him in a snaffle in the morning, letting him have a good look around. You simply cannot arrive at a show, get on board and work him. Submission straight off would be totally impossible. He has to look at everything, and then I put him away after he has thought about what he has seen. When he has got a feel for his surroundings then I can bring him out and work him in for his test. At this point I am not fighting the mental part because he has had a chance to

Here I am concentrating on the contact with Dolendo.

acclimatise. In the early days I would try to prevent him from looking and it made him worse. He would get really tense, his breathing would get heavy and then all he wanted to do was gawp. However, once he had had a look he was fine.

So at shows be prepared to hack your horse around. Give it a long rein, and let it walk around and take in the sights. This is especially important for nosey horses like Donald and Peanuts, who are not relaxed if they do not know what is around them. They need to feel comfortable in their surroundings and you have to give them time, by walking them on a long rein, to relax them and let them take everything in.

Some riders get obsessed about having the horse on the bit immediately upon arrival at the show, so they argue and try to keep the horse's head down. To do this they pull on the mouth, which then creates tension and causes a 'lock-jaw' effect on the horse. The result is that the horse becomes very stiff and hard because it is not relaxed, and because the rider is holding it down rather than riding it in balance. Balance does not mean having the horse's head down – and that is a trap that many inexperienced people fall into.

Santas, who has been with us now for over a year, is an interesting case who has proved surprisingly difficult to get to know. A small tour horse, he arrived as a well-trained ride ready to compete and already conversant with piaffe, passage and one-time changes. He was a willing individual and did what he was told, which might lead you to think that you could get to know him well within two or three months. However, it has taken me over a year to be able to feel that I can mould him to how I want. I finally achieved it by getting him fitter and riding him in a faster rhythm.

Horses like Santas tend to get stuck in their preferred (and somewhat laid-back) rhythm. I have had to spend a lot of time riding him up-tempo and out of his rhythm to try and get him to tune in to me rather than me fitting to him. This was the main work as everything else was very secure.

He is also a horse that cannot be ridden for too long, otherwise he starts to depend on the rider to carry him and he gets heavy and lazy. This then shows up, for example, as irregularities in half-pass, through leaning too much on the bit.

For Santas, it has been a question of getting him quicker and lighter. As a result he has been transformed into a horse with Grand Prix carriage, whereas he previously just looked a nice, level horse. It is a matter of getting extra 'spark' into his work. The next job will be getting the 'spark' into his tests!

To achieve extra fitness he has done a lot of cantering and a lot of sharp, fast work. This highlights the fact that because warmbloods generally lack the Thoroughbred element they may have to be trained more like an eventer. His type needs to develop the carrying, the pushing and the speed, unlike the hotter types who need to spend time in a relaxed and stretched position. So establishing the rhythm in these 'colder' horses at four and five is fine, but once this is established and they reach six or seven they need to work harder and faster.

Riding the Big Movers

It is important not to let a big-moving horse always move big. This is one problem I had with Peanuts which I have never had with Pro Set, for example. Peanuts has always wanted to move like a Grand Prix horse, whereas Pro is one that I will teach to move that way. As a result I mostly keep Peanuts in a working trot so he saves himself.

Big movers can sometimes have no real engagement as young horses, so they have to learn to move less extravagantly to be in real balance. In the same way, the small movers have to learn to let go and move bigger.

As a rider and trainer I find these horses particularly interesting simply because they are so different. The secret of their success is that despite their different shapes, sizes and temperaments when they are trained to take into account their own individual needs, as with any other horse, it is possible to get the best out of them.

Fizzy Horses

'Hot' horses need patient handling, and a routine is all-important. An ideal training session for a very hot horse would be to warm him up, do some work on his difficult, problem areas, and then make a mental note to finish off on the things you know he can do well and enjoys.

Fizzy horses need to be submissive enough to allow themselves to be ridden, which can only come about as a result of a good, trusting relationship with their rider. They cannot perform if nervous or quashed by the rider.

Riders need patience and should be prepared to drop down a level in competition in order to obtain the submission and confidence they require from their horse. If necessary, go back to basics sometimes and take the pressure off the horse by returning to simple stretching exercises in a snaffle bridle or by just hacking for a week.

Be prepared to go to a few shows before you start to compete to get your horse used to being out and about. At international shows it is possible to arrive a few days before the event, and this is always useful.

Give your Horse a Break

Horses don't have to be schooled every day – they need holidays too. Don't worry that your horse will forget everything it has been taught. It won't. When a horse is relaxed it is amazing just how much it will pick up. Hacking and regular turn-out relieve stress. Variety is the key, so get your horse out doing different things.

Dolendo being encouraged to express himself after doing something particularly well.

Chapter Four

Further Philosophy – For Young Horses

Young horses need time, patience and understanding. If these three elements are combined with the structure of the scales of training, a young horse stands a good chance of getting to the top.

Testing for Potential

When I ride our four-year-olds I like to 'test the water' by asking a few questions. For example, I might try out a flying change, or tap the hindquarter lightly with the whip, or ask for a bigger trot. At this stage I am just looking to see how trainable the horse is. I am not wanting to push the horse as I want to preserve its soundness for its career.

An interesting observation came to light when testing Dolendo and Groove Jet as youngsters. Both were big movers but lacked engagement; however, they were naturals when it came to moving sideways. On the whole, longer horses do go sideways more easily than shorter ones, while shorter horses may find it easier to piaffe and passage than the longer horses. It all goes back to conformation, and longer horses finding it more difficult to engage (as their hind legs have further to travel under their body due to their length of back). Different conformations have their strengths and weaknesses and this is where the trainer has to see what he has to train. In other words, what the horse has been blessed with and where he will need help in training. It is a question of assessing what aspects are not ideal and then thinking about what you can do to improve them.

The Importance of Transitions

Transitions are all about the process of stopping, starting, changing pace and the use of the half-halt. They are the stepping stones to further development, improved paces, and they get horses thinking. They also play a role in submission, obedience and gaining the horse's attention.

A three-and-a-half-year-old, showing the importance of lungeing the young horse to develop strength.

Stopping and Starting

In the beginning the use of the rein must be established before combining leg and rein together in a more subtle way. Eventually your rein, seat and leg aids communicate together, but at an early stage the horse does not understand that. The forward aid pushes the horse into the hand, and at some stage, with some horses, this is where you could have problems. This is because if you are using too much leg and hand at that level, the horse gets dead to the leg and pulls on the rein because you are pushing it against the hand. If the horse has not understood what the rein is for he is going to pull, and so the rider creates a dead mouth and loses the lightness or the speed to react.

Initially horses must learn that the rein is to come back and the leg is to go – so when you touch them with the leg they go, and when you give the aid with the reins, they come back to you. At this level you should maintain the forward movement with the hand. I prefer not to push with my leg in the downward transition because this will give a conflicting aid. It is only at a later stage of training that you will use the leg to push the horse into the contact. The aids get more subtle as the horse becomes more established in its work.

With hotter young horses like Superman, and Peanuts when he was that age, you need to spend a lot more time 'stopping' rather than 'going', because you have to reach the point where you can put your legs on and ride them. When they do not understand the rein aids, because they are young, they will run with you and just keep running until you end up either pulling to stop them or not being able to teach them anything because they are always tearing away from you. With these types of horses you spend more time on the transitions downwards, repeating the 'stopping' process until they have learned about the rein aid. And you cannot get them to accept the leg unless they learn the rein aid.

For lazier types of horse you still use a lot of 'stopping' and 'starting', but it is the 'starting' that would be more important. You need to get them off your leg.

It is important to remember, though, that with a young horse you do not have to spend a lot of time trotting and cantering thereby exhausting it. If you ride it longer because it is a hotter type then you can spend more time walking and halting, over and over, just to establish attention from the horse through your aids. A lazy horse, however, would need to be kept sharp and keen for 15 to 20 minutes.

Moving Young Horses Sideways

It is common for young horses, in the early days, to lean in, particularly on corners and turns, for balance. As a result the rider feels like he is on 'the wall of death', particularly when the horse is in canter. Basically the young horse does not understand the importance of being supported by the inside leg, so this is something you will have to address. The way to do this is to introduce it to leg-yield, or perhaps a little shoulder-in on the circle, so eventually it learns to bend through its body and connect with the outside rein. Once this is established you start to translate that to circles and turns. Having learned about 'stopping' and 'starting', the horse must then learn to move sideways off the leg so that it understands what yielding is.

It is important to stress at this stage that the various forms of leg-yielding are not collected lateral movements because the horse is only flexed away from the bend, and does not need to be collected. A rider needs to differentiate between leg-yielding and shoulder-in.

Leg-yielding is an exercise for developing looseness. It makes the horse more responsive to the sideways-pushing aids. It is an excellent exercise for teaching the rider to coordinate the aids. The horse moves forwards and sideways on two tracks with a slight flexion of the head and neck, but with only limited bend through its body. The inside feet step regularly and evenly in front of and across the outside feet. The flexion is always to the side of the sideways-pushing leg. The sideways-pushing leg is therefore the inside leg, even when it is on the side closest to the wall.

I find the leg-yield very useful, but there are some who do not believe in it. They argue that it is unnecessary to teach the horse leg-yield when you then have to teach it half-pass. My answer to that is why not teach them both because they have to learn to bend in different directions? It is much easier for a young horse to move away from the direction of the bend, and leg-yield is not a collecting movement; it is, in fact, a free forward movement. This is in contrast to the half-pass, where the horse has to bend and engage his hind leg more, thus making it a collected movement.

I use a lot of leg-yield, and I even do leg-yield in canter too. I don't see it being practised much elsewhere, and is not required in a test, but as a training aid I think it's a brilliant exercise.

Should Youngsters do Stretching Exercises?

Riders need to be aware that for youngsters stretching over the back is an exercise in itself, while for older horses it is a form of cooling down.

Young horses do need some stretching-down work, but at this stage not too much. The amount will depend on the natural balance of the horse. The rider teaches the horse to be ridden on the bit because it is a very natural place for him to be balanced at a young age. Moreover this is what is required of him in a test situation or young horse class. Youngsters are expected to carry themselves on the bit, albeit to a novice degree, and their breaks in schooling should come through walking and allowing them to stretch and have a breather. At this age they are generally not strong enough to stretch over their back and remain engaged, which is the important part of stretching. It is not a question of putting the horse on the forehand. Superman, Groove Jet and Pro Set have all learned to stretch and stay engaged and I use this a lot in their work to get them soft and to make them more supple as they have become stronger. Inexperienced riders need to be aware that horses are not strong enough for this initially. If you stretched a young horse for ten minutes that would be its work done for the day and it would be exhausted, whereas for older horses it is part of their relaxation during their training sessions.

Superman, although too deep for my liking, is following the hand.

Common Problems with Young Horses

Most of the problems are contact problems and they manifest themselves in various ways. One example would be when the horse does not accept the leg or rein aids. Horses can often be more crooked when they are younger so when a rider gets a horse that 'leans over', which can also involve the twisting of the head and neck, it must be corrected immediately. A rider can do this by forward riding and making sure that the horse is even on both reins. Also at this point it is time to start teaching suppleness through lateral work.

If you have an excitable horse it is helpful to work on what it is good at from time to time, in between the problems, as this has a settling effect. However, I do believe that you must take a disciplined approach to addressing any problem. Be prepared to stick with it and see it through, and always finish on a good note. Remember, too, not to finish up any session with exercises the horse struggles with. Interestingly, a lot of problems often come right when you leave them, for example when you first teach flying changes. They get worse if you keep hammering away at them, and very often it is good to attempt the changes, leave them for a few days, and then come back to them, and they start

Superman stretching, but the stretch is not perfect. The tail is up, and the back is up and swinging, but I would like him to open up more in the bottom of his neck so that his back behind the saddle really gets a full stretch.

Superman. This is the **preferred stretch** for a young horse.

to sort themselves out as the horse starts to think as well as strengthen.

'Contact' problems must not always be associated with the horse being difficult as a lot of the time the horse simply is not strong enough to carry itself evenly. The potential lack of strength of the young horse must always be considered, especially if it is a big horse. The rider also has to take into account how the horse is built and its movement. Does it have a naturally 'engaged' hind leg? Is it slow behind? Is it heavier at the front at this stage because it is not coming up through the forehand. These are all points which have to be considered on an on-going basis.

Spooking

Spooking is something that I am often asked about. My feeling is that if you push the horse very positively towards whatever it is that has upset him, then you will create a big problem. Your horse will become stiff with a very hard mouth. You need to take time and let the horse look, while walking around letting it put its head where it wants to. It is a mistake to get too dressage-orientated, thinking that the horse must be on the bit all the time. Give the horse time to relax its body; that way its jaw relaxes and so does the hand contact. For a young spooky horse that doesn't have a lot of 'work' energy in it, riding it forward under these conditions is not the answer. It is better to spend time in walk until you can get the horse to move around from your leg again. This is where the leg-yielding, or the submission to moving away from your leg, can be so useful. If you can move the horse sideways towards the object it is spooking at, while you keep it flexed away from it, then you stand a much better chance of getting there.

Certain individuals (like Peanuts) are not actually spooky but inattentive. Sometimes you have to make allowances and compromise (I had to let Peanuts look at whatever it was that was that had caught his eye – if I didn't, I could feel his breathing start to increase and his neck tighten), but, of course, you hope that as the horse gets older these situations won't arise so frequently. You must find a balance between letting them have a look but not letting them get away with things.

Take, for instance, the problem of a horse that won't go into a corner. Work near the corner, walk through the corner, let the horse stand in the corner, or rein it back towards the corner. Try all the different options, but do not let the horse get away with it. Very often a young horse will follow another horse into the corner. It's a matter of confidence, which is built up by repetition rather than reprimand. Once confidence is built up at home then the horse can go to its first show.

Spooky horses are difficult to deal with but there are many things that you can do. For instance, a rider can take a horse out to new places, borrow arenas, ride with other horses, and generally encourage horses to go in the ring before they compete, giving them a chance to look around. Shows are not there to catch horses out. Shows act as an aid and a guide to a horse's development and training. If you have a particular problem with an arena then you must stay until the end of the day and ask if you can take the horse back into the arena. If you haven't got time, then hire the venue another day or borrow a friend's arena.

> The key to solving any problems is to persevere.

Chapter Five

Training the Four- and Five-Year-Olds

At this stage the most important things are that the paces are regular and unhurried, and that balance and rhythm are maintained with the horse in a natural rounded outline, without him being restricted. The horse should move freely forward without collection but with active hindquarters. He should accept the bit willingly and without tension or resistance, and he should be calm, relaxed and obedient to the aids of the rider. Finally the horse must be straight on straight lines, and bent when moving on curves. He should also have smooth transitions and remain still when halted. If, when schooling and competing, a horse masters all these things consistently, then it is ready to move on to the next stage.

SUPERMAN (5 years)

I first saw Superman (aged four) on a trip to Holland, with Sandra Biddlecombe. He reminded me of a dachshund because he had a big body and short legs. The things that stood out about him were his intelligence and exuberant nature.

Generally, riders 'make' mouths as they train horses, but Superman was blessed with a very good mouth which was, and still is, very soft and closed, making him easy to ride on the bit. Most four- or five-year-olds have to be taught to go on the bit but Superman does it naturally.

I saw him loose-schooled, and Sandra Biddlecombe bought him. Superman shows a fantastic degree of suppleness and softness in his movement, and he has an outstanding canter. He has a very high foreleg action, naturally engaged hind legs, and an uphill, loose, extravagant trot. I could feel there was something quite extraordinary about Superman's trot, although from the ground it did not look all that amazing. It was the type of trot that I felt, with training, you could make very special.

It is a good idea when you see a horse loose in a school, to ask to have all whips, bags and people removed from the school so you can assess the normal trot and canter without distractions. The walk is also important. Superman's walk is not huge but it is very correct and never out of rhythm.

Superman's work so far has involved nothing more than basic walk, trot and canter around a school. It is all he has needed to do because he is so balanced and on the bit. As he has such natural exuberance and desire to go forward, the main aim to date has been to maintain the rhythm and keep encouraging him with his forwardness. He also hacks out and goes in the field, where he also shows off his natural 'joie de vivre'.

The good thing about a small, compact horse like Superman (he's 15.3 hh) is that you are dealing with a horse that is already physically very strong. He has a good neck and hindquarter and is naturally engaged, so it's just been a question of keeping him relaxed because everything else comes to him easily. He has

Superman, epitomising a novice horse working correctly. He has a very open jaw line, and his hind legs are swinging through and making a nice track-up. Relaxation is further shown by the fact that the neck is very round and not wrinkled because it is uptight.

Superman, in his natural shape, easy on the bit and with good paces. He has learned about the contact and has found his balance, so he is secure in his work.

everything that one looks for when going to buy a young horse. He is not spooky, but he has enough hotness to give the feeling that there is something special there. Every now and again when you pick up the whip with him and do a 'little bit extra' he starts to move like a Grand Prix horse and he feels at least 17.2 hands high. This I would only do once a week. It is exciting to know that this potential is there, but the rest of the time we concentrate on the stretching, suppling and softness that builds up the right muscles.

Superman has now started leg-yielding and this helps him especially when he goes to shows. We found that he became more excitable at competitions and would not accept the leg because he was so keen. Normally at home he is very rideable, but with the crowds and the clapping he tended to go over the top. It is important not to wear the horse out but instead to give him exercises such as turning him around your leg and moving him sideways. This work does not allow him to run forward, away from the leg.

Something that Superman does need to spend a lot of time on are transitions. Big-moving horses make big transitions, which sometimes upset the balance, so it is a question of working on easy, smaller transitions and trying the whole time to get the canter smoother. I have to teach him that he does not have to throw his head and neck up to get into canter, but because he is in such a big trot he naturally goes into a big canter.

Superman is just starting out in his training and although he is a supremely gifted horse, his regime is about establishing the basics, just as for any horse of his age. It is important, however, to remember the scales of training, and the first goal on the list – rhythm. Superman is worked with this in mind and he starts his sessions with rising trot just to get him looser in his back to get his outline a bit softer and a bit lower. As he works on softening and stretching exercises it is important to feel him stretch and soften over the back and to watch the tail come up and swing when he is really stretching. The work is never hurried and at all times he is encouraged to stay in rhythm.

Training Advice

Different Forms of Stretching Over the Back

The value of stretching cannot be over-emphasised, and the type of stretching work I do depends very much on the horse. For any such work it is very important that the horse has learned to go on the bit with a contact. For horses such as Hector and Donald, their work is deeper and rounder with an arch over the top line, since they have a tendency to take a strong contact. These are big horses who need to keep their top line soft. Working in a stretched outline keeps the horse supple and as light as possible in the rein. The sort of contact the horse takes influences the type of stretching I would do with that individual. Horses that are more naturally balanced can work with greater length over their back.

For horses that are less submissive, the more stretching over the back they do, the looser they become in the hand. For those horses that are more naturally relaxed and balanced, it is more a matter of longitudinal stretching over the back, which of course, is the ultimate aim for all horses.

Sometimes it is better to make the horse submissive by bringing him in a little bit deeper and then letting him out as he lets go, rather than letting him put his nose out, which will result in him going against the bit and pulling down onto the forehand, which causes the hind legs to go out at the back. It is important to remember that stretching is all about keeping the wither up and not flattening the horse in front.

The rider needs to ensure that there is an arc over the whole of the horse's top line. The arc starts with the head and runs over the back, with the hocks underneath, so making a lovely round shape. The outline of the arc will depend on the size and shape of the horse. The shorter types, like Superman, need to be stretched to make their body longer because they are short and more muscular, whereas the longer horses, who are not always easy to keep together and can go more against the hand, need to have that deeper roundness to keep them more engaged when they are stretching. Hector is a good example of the latter.

Deep, round stretching as opposed to the longer stretching (shown below).

Longitudinal stretching with everything working correctly as it should. It is important to note that the rider's hand position is slightly lower than normal to encourage the bit to be slightly lower in the horse's mouth. This is achieved by a little massaging on the rein just to get the horse to follow the bit softly.

Hector feels better in a deeper frame, although he looks more overbent because of his physique. If he was let out in front he would also go out behind, which would result in a completely 'strung-out' frame. Keeping him deeper in front means that it is easier for me to keep his hind legs under in the stretching as he is not pulling against the hand.

Everything coming together, with Superman **canter-stretching** in balance.

Pitfalls of Stretching

Riders must be sure to avoid the following when stretching the horse:

- ▓ Be aware that, to a certain extent, a young horse will be more on the forehand when stretching as it has not developed real engagement.

- ▓ The horse must not be tight on the rein and held overbent. If the horse is held in the stretch, or, alternatively, if it is overbent against the hand, then the rider is effectively riding with the handbrake on and as a result the hind legs will not come underneath the horse.

- ▓ The horse should not change gear. It should not, when the rider gives the rein, run off or speed up. A horse that is really in balance will put its head and neck down and stay at the same pace. This is a true sign of self-carriage. When the reins are given, the horse lowers and rounds without speeding up.

■ The horse must not be allowed to drop the bit in his stretching. The horse must always be following the hand, whether deeper or longer. It must not be heavy in the hand, or not in the hand at all. In other words, the horse must not come in and drop the bit, nor must it go out and pull on the bit. It must follow the hand down and make an arc, and the way each horse does this will be different according to its shape and size.

The rider's feel plays an important role here as sometimes it will tell him to have the horse a little deeper because it gives a nicer feeling in the hand. However, this must not be confused with having the horse behind the bit. This is why, when trying a potential dressage horse with a view to buying, it is vital to get on and feel it because your feeling will give you the answers to questions such as: Is it in front of the leg? Does it want to go? Does the horse have swing? You cannot always see these things from the ground, but you can feel them.

It goes without saying that the rider's leg is all-important when stretching the horse. Through feel the rider must know when to use the leg as a 'forward' aid and when to use it in conjunction with the reins, to ask the horse to bring its hind legs under and to collect, thereby using the half-halt, which has the effect of elevating the horse. When you release the rein and use your leg, the horse knows to go forward.

> When stretching the horse down, feel is everything. It is all about soft, supple riding, not riding with the handbrake on.

I believe horses benefit from being stretched, but if you feel stretching is not right for you or your horse, that's fine. I can only speak from my own experience and what I feel as a rider.

Whether you are riding at preliminary level or Grand Prix, the outline – appropriate to that particular level of the horse's training and for riding that particular test – must be right. For me, as a rider and trainer, the most important things are the bending, the suppling and the stretching. A rider must also learn to understand how to ride a horse 'on the bit' as this too is vital to the training and competing of the horse. The ideal would be to produce a supple, obedient horse who, through correct schooling, started out at three years old and was able to go on to twenty-three.

Half-Halt

There are three degrees of the half-halt. It can be used:

■ For the full halt – as in the 'stopping and starting' exercise for young horses.

■ For changes in the pace – in other words, the gears.

■ Invisibly, when the rider's leg, seat and rein work together to achieve movements such as piaffe and pirouettes, with lightness and ease.

In the early stages of a horse's career, the half-halt is employed actually to halt the horse. Then, as the horse understands the request, the next step is to use the half-halt to 'change gear' in the pace. Finally, the ultimate half-halt is used in Grand Prix, when the horse piaffes. A rider might apply half-halts before movements, within paces and in transitions between paces.

The half-halt is very much down to the rider's own feel – and everyone is different. It is applied via the rider's seat, legs and rein aid, and should be as invisible as possible. The idea is to gain the horse's attention and put his balance more on the hind leg. By shifting more weight onto the horse's hind legs and engaging them this way you improve his balance and attain lightness in the forehand, which enables the horse to move in self-carriage.

The half-halt itself is a difficult process to describe. It is a moment – a hesitation – which you have to catch, usually by bracing the back and releasing it as you feel the horse come back to you. In other words, you almost stop then go forward again. At the top end of the scale, in the case of piaffe, when the horse wants to go forward, you check it with a light rein aid, and the hind legs come under and so it piaffes. Timing is of the essence with the half-halt.

The half-halt, as Superman is brought back in the trot. It all happens so fleetingly, but looking at photos, you can see that the horse has started to bring his hind leg up rather than push it forward and so start to shift the weight back onto his hind leg. This is done either in preparation to shorten the stride or possibly to make a transition to walk. It is interesting to note the length in the horse's frame – this is very important because the horse balances himself with his neck, so he needs to have this long neck in the transitions.

Training Tip

Half-halts are done from the early stages of training right up to Grand Prix and they can be done simultaneously, one after the other, until the rider has the desired attention and lightness. Half-halts are vital if you want to carry out movements with lightness and ease.

Chapter Six

Training the Six- and Seven-Year-Olds

Once the basics set out in the previous chapter are established, the rider can move on to the next stage. Now, greater muscular development, suppleness and impulsion are sought in order that the horse can execute with ease the more demanding movements of tests at this higher level (elementary). A slightly higher, rounded outline than at novice is required as a result of increased engagement of the hind legs; and while collection is asked for, riders are only expected to show sufficient engagement to carry out the required movements.

The contact between the rider's hand and the horse's mouth should be strengthened further, with a soft and steady contact on both reins. The horse's submission to weight, leg and rein aids increases primarily in the forward-driving and regulating aids to achieve 'throughness', or the state of being 'through'. Throughness leads to the strengthening of the muscles in the hindquarters so that they can carry more weight; this in turn takes the weight off the forehand giving the shoulder greater freedom.

PRO SET (7 years)

Pro Set is a wiry little stallion. At seven years old he is already showing some piaffe, passage and one-time changes. He is lively and enthusiastic, almost to the point of getting himself very tense, especially at shows, but he is, without a doubt, the type of horse I like. He needs reassurance from his rider, and it is definitely a question of whoa not go! Having said that, he is not a spooky horse.

He is a different type completely to Superman, being built like a whippet with no muscle as yet, and he naturally becomes more hyped-up in the breeding season. Every year he has to take time out from training for his stud duties between March and June because he cannot cope with both at once. He is a supremely intelligent horse and never has any trouble with the movements, beginning to show a little bit of everything already. He has a huge trot, yet has a wonderful ability to collect too. However, his back is potentially his weak area, but this is something that has to be borne in mind with all stallions because of covering mares. All horses need to be strong in their backs for their work and Pro Set is no exception. As a result he needs to spend a lot of time in a very stretched position to get his back muscles really built up.

So far, his competition record is fantastic. With a horse like this, his stud duties being a priority, we have to take things one step at a time, but to date he shows all the ability of a Grand Prix stallion so we do not mind how long it takes because he has so much going for him.

He is a spirited ride, and like all stallions, if you tackle his tension in a dominating way he can become very argumentative, but despite those moments he is very much a stallion that is in tune with his rider. It is best with stallions to get them into a routine when it comes to work. I always ride Pro Set first every day. This means that I ride him in peace and quiet, when there are no other horses in the school; I can make him submissive and he is very happy to work. Through this routine, my hope is that Pro will become so obedient to the work that ultimately his obedience will overcome his desire not to concentrate. Certainly if I had ridden him with other horses in the initial stages of his training he would never have worked or learned anything I was trying to teach him. However, once settled in a routine I can achieve a great deal.

It is always a good idea with very energetic young horses to lunge them or turn them loose in a sand school to let off steam, therefore reducing the risk of arguments when it comes to buckling down to work. Hacking out with a stallion such as Pro Set is not a good idea, but we can use the other ways to help him lose excess energy, allowing him to be relaxed when we need him to be.

Training Advice

When working a horse between elementary and advanced medium, the basic requirements are the same. That is to say, all movements 'have to be performed with ease'. The easier a rider makes it look, the more likely they are to win. The one thing a rider has to remember is not to sacrifice the horse's paces at these levels. At elementary level you are at an 'in between' stage, perhaps with a horse that needs to learn to move or is not strong enough, so each horse must be worked accordingly. When working at elementary a high degree of obedience and some collection is required, together with more expression of movement. Even a naturally forward-going horse ridden by a professional will need at least two years training to reach this standard comfortably.

The rider must first establish the basics and then allow the horse to mature. Superman, because of the size of his movement, would need at least another year before he would be proficient at elementary level. Escapado did his first elementary at six years old. Novice and elementary tests are very well designed to give a rider an indication as to when a horse is ready to move up to the next level. They are sufficiently testing to prevent you from rushing up to the next level.

Medium and Advanced Medium are a big step up, so horses must be well established in novice and elementary first. The rider must be able to execute the movements correctly and precisely, employing less obvious aids than previously. The horse has to show equal development on both sides through lateral movements, demonstrate the ability to carry out flying changes in canter, while working with increased collection and greater expression. The horse should show improved paces and outline, plus suppleness and impulsion to collect and extend its paces when receiving the aids.

■ Exercises

Transitions

Once the horse has become established in the core work and understands the basic half-halt, then transitions become a very important part of the daily work.

A rider needs to practise as many transitions as possible to get the horse to push in the upward transitions and to get the hind legs to come under in the downward transitions. When schooling, the rider needs to think in terms of some fifty to sixty transitions per session at least, although the horse's age and strength must also be taken into account. The work on the transitions should see the shoulder start to elevate and the carrying power develop behind.

Leg-Yielding

As previously mentioned this is an exercise aimed at developing looseness (*losgelassenheit*) and making the horse responsive to the sideways-pushing aids. It also helps riders with co-ordination.

Leg-yielding is often taught before shoulder-in to make the horse more aware of the inside leg aids. It teaches the horse to yield to increased pressure from the rider's leg placed on the girth, from which he (the horse) must move away. It is used to increase bend or lighten the weight of the horse when falling in on a corner or

A good exercise is to ride leg-yield on the centre line to the quarter line, then move into shoulder-in on the quarter line (see also photo sequence overleaf).

In this photo Spencer can be seen getting Pro off the inside leg and working shoulder-in away from the wall, which really tells the rider if he has the horse truly on the outside rein. There is a debate with shoulder-in as to whether it should be on three or four tracks. I use three tracks as I feel it is a better angle.

Riding it on the quarter line enables you to feel more easily whether there is too much angle, which is a problem that occurs a lot on the long side. It is important to ride the leg-yield very much **from the leg and with a very soft rein**, thus preventing pulling the horse around into position with the rein.

on a circle. It is also useful for engaging the horse's hind leg prior to asking him to go forwards with greater impulsion. Often it is first taught on a line parallel to the side of the school, asking the horse to leg-yield to the track. Once learned, it can be carried out in a variety of places. The horse's bend should be very slightly away from the direction he is going in.

A nice sequence showing Spencer just turning Pro's front end more to the inside to make shoulder-in after the leg-yield.

Shoulder-In

This movement is the backbone of all lateral work and is very important in making the young horse straight. The horse's hind legs remain on the outside track while the forehand is brought just enough to the inside that the horse's outside shoulder is in front of his inside hip. The horse's inside foreleg passes and crosses in front of the outside leg; the inside leg is placed in front of the outside leg. From the front we see three tracks. The horse is bent and flexed laterally away from the direction in which he is moving.

It is a very valuable exercise for the rider as the diagonal aids can be used to improve the horse's straightness. By this I mean that the rider drives the inside leg against the outside controlling rein therefore straightening the horse relative to himself.

If this exercise is done correctly, with the horse slightly bent round the inside leg of the rider, and at the correct angle, it is not only a suppling movement but also a collecting movement, as the horse at every step must move his inside hind leg underneath his body and place it in front of the outside, which he is unable to do without lowering his inside hip.

ABOVE: An incorrect shoulder-in. The horse is being taken onto four tracks, and at this point the rider has over-turned the horse to the inside. As a result, the horse is falling through the left shoulder rather than remaining straighter and staying on the outside rein, and on three tracks.

LEFT: A correct shoulder-in. Spencer has done the movement again to correct the fault shown above. This illustrates why riding quarter lines is so good for the rider, because you really have control of the horse with your seat, leg and rein.

Travers down the long side, illustrating the position of the hindquarters and demonstrating the support the side of the school gives, making the movement easier for the horse before it moves on to the diagonal and the half-pass.

Travers

This movement is performed with the horse flexed and bent in the direction in which he is moving. The forehand remains on the outside track while the hindquarters are moved to the inside. From the front the horse can be seen to be on four tracks. It is often taught before half-pass on the diagonal. It is the same

Having just done travers down the long side, Pro is now coming across the diagonal. As this is a young horse I let him trail slightly with the hindquarters, and he is not encouraged to be parallel because sometimes when you make them parallel, at that early stage, they lose the quality of the trot. I always prioritise the quality of the trot, so letting him trail slightly is acceptable at this stage of his training.

An exercise which ensures the stride stays good. The rider does medium trot on the diagonal towards X, and then at X rides into travers towards the corner. By riding medium trot first, which can be seen head-on in this photo, the rider freshens up the stride getting the stride really big and the horse in front of the leg. Then the travers that you ride into at X collects the horse.

Riding into travers from the medium trot.

exercise but is performed along the wall or on the centre line at an angle of 30° to the direction in which the horse is moving. The wall helps the rider control the bend and maintain the angle, thus making it easier than the half-pass on the diagonal where there is no distinct line.

Counter Canter

This movement requires good balance. It is most important that the horse has learned how to maintain the same three-beat rhythm and does not sacrifice the movement. Remember that the horse should not be ridden so deeply into the corners, and that the forehand and the hindquarters remain on the same track. The horse is then flexed to the side of the leading leg. The aids are the same as in a normal canter but the rider must not collapse the inside hip; he must also sit in balance, so maintaining the horse's balance. The rider must lighten or give the inside rein (it is responsible for the flexion) so that the inside hind leg of the horse can step under sufficiently; and as with the normal canter, the horse must remain on the outside rein.

Reminders for Counter Canter

- Keep the weight over the leading leg
- Keep the outside leg back
- Maintain the canter with the inside leg
- Do not lose the bend to the leading leg
- Despite keeping the bend, do not restrict the pace with the inside rein
- Do not alter direction suddenly

A counter-canter exercise, with medium canter on the long sides in counter canter, and really using the corner to get the horse to stretch through – because the canter hind leg is on the outside. This exercise shows how much stretching the horse needs, and by using the impulsion from the medium canter on the long side it creates a really good three-beat in the counter canter.

Quarter Pirouettes

It is possible to start to introduce the idea of a pirouette to a horse at this stage by riding quarter pirouettes. It is a good method of teaching the horse from the start to respect the rider's inside leg, and not to throw itself into the turn. The rider must be able to feel whether the horse is stepping forward sufficiently under its centre of gravity, or whether its quarters are escaping to the outside. The rider must also bear in mind the fact that these exercises, particularly for young horses, require considerable effort and so should not be practised to excess.

Pro and Spencer tackling a quarter pirouette/travers exercise. Here the horse is asked to do travers down the long side, collect before the corner, do a quarter pirouette, travers to the other side of the school, collect, quarter pirouette and travers again.

Here we see Pro really bent round the inside leg, and starting to make his quarter turn. Ideally I would like the rider to have more contact on the outside rein to bring the shoulder round more. The horse is coming slightly too much to the inside and leaning over.

Another attempt at the quarter pirouette/travers exercise. In this sequence Pro is starting to make a quarter pirouette in which Spencer is not asking for a great deal of collection because Pro is a young horse. We are just asking the horse to bring his shoulders around his hind legs.

Half-Pass (Young Horses)

Once travers is established on both reins then half-pass should not be a problem. The bend of the half-pass differs from that in leg-yield and is more difficult for the horse. The exercise gives more freedom and mobility to the shoulders; because it demands more suppleness, the outcome should be greater ease of movement.

When teaching the horse half-pass be prepared for the quarters to trail slightly as it will maintain the forward movement. Initially use the long diagonal for half-pass, but be aware of just how strenuous this exercise is and make sure it is

developed slowly. Only when the horse is strong and confident sideways can you make him really parallel and ask for steeper angles. In tests it is usually from the centre line to the side or vice versa, to encourage riders to work forwards in their half-passes. Once in Grand Prix, half-pass is much steeper. Horses should be able to cross from one side of the school to the other then back again. To assess progress, follow a checklist:

- Is the trot in the same forward rhythm sideways and in a straight line?

- Does the horse stay balanced?

- Does the rider have the correct bend?

Weight into the inside heel

The rider needs to put weight more into the inside heel to encourage the horse to step in that direction. Try leaning right over to the inside to see if you can see the outside hind leg crossing over. This sometimes helps you to sit into and feel the direction of the movement the horse is travelling in, instead of tending to sit to the outside, which is a common fault. It will help you to understand the use of weight as an aid.

Four steps at a time

When first starting in half-pass ride four steps to the side, then four straight, then four to the side, in a sequence. This enables you to keep control of the horse and the aids, and gives time to correct faults, such as quarters leading or trailing, before they become established. Quarters leading is the result of either too much or too little bend, which is a control and balance problem.

Here Spencer has ridden a half-pass to the centre line, before making a 10-metre circle of travers; then, having completed the 10-metre circle in travers, he continues in half-pass again, using the whole of the long line on the diagonal to do the exercise. You can, for example, ride this exercise: F–X half-pass, at X ride a 10-metre circle of travers, and then ride X to H in half-pass again. This gives the horse a feel of what is to come.

An excellent picture which shows the horse on the long side, moving from travers into a quarter pirouette.

Half-pass to circle back to half-pass

Try riding half-pass to the left, followed by a 10-metre circle right, followed by half-pass right, and vice versa. Through this exercise the rider stays in control of the horse's balance and prevents any anticipation on the horse's part. This, it should be emphasised, is a trot exercise.

Canter Pirouettes

In the case of Pro and Hector, who are just learning about canter pirouettes, we use a 'half-pass, big circle, half-pass' exercise and also ride long sides in travers, with little quarter turns at the end just to give them an indication of what is to come. With a younger horse doing these for the first time, the rider has to feel his way through a test. Horses tend to be more tense at competitions, especially at an earlier age when they are a bit more nervous or distracted, so with less-

Pro Set mastering the art of the pirouette, but at this stage of his training, as you can see from the photo, we are encouraging more forward strides around a 10-metre circle in travers.

experienced horses ride larger pirouettes to try to teach them the safety of the stride.

The exercises covered in this chapter follow a logical progression as the horse develops and gains strength. Once mastered it is possible to go on to the next stage . . .

Chapter Seven

Training the Seven- and Eight-Year-Olds

At this level (medium/advanced medium) it is possible to distinguish between the training to reach a particular level, as in the case of Pro Set in the previous chapter, and then moving on to reinforce what has been learned until the required movements can be carried out independently. Here, among other objectives, I aim to ensure equal development of the horse on both sides through lateral movements. I start exercises such as the flying change, seek to increase collection and look to achieve greater expression in the horse's action while aiming to get the horse to present himself more naturally.

GROOVE JET (8 years)

I bought Groove Jet (aka Hector) as an 'heir and a spare', and he was the spare! As a foal he was big, bold and had a huge trot, and he definitely stood out in the group of foals I went to see.

When I am looking at foals I like to see them move quite slowly, not at top speed because that gives a false impression. When I look at a foal I try to imagine a miniature horse and assess it for potential top line, hind-leg movement and the ability to swing without having to go fast.

Timid horses are often good horses because they have to put their trust in you. Having said that, I bought Hector because he came striding over to me

from out of the group and said, 'I will come with you.' There were no ifs or buts; he had simply decided. I, in turn, thought how lovely he looked, and took him home. At that time (some eight years ago) I did not pay much attention to conformation or type. I liked his breeding, and as foals were relatively inexpensive, he was not a huge financial risk. So far he is looking good!

At an early age he was a great big lump with big movement and he kept on tripping over his legs as he simply could not cope. His movement undoubtedly won him the Novice championships. As he has matured he has found his balance and everything has started to come together. Over the last four years Spencer and I have given him a little taste of all the Grand Prix movements, but he has been taken slowly because of his size. He is very gangly with long legs, long body, long neck and a slow brain. He was a lazy, unenthusiastic youngster, and when he was four, and I was kicking and shoving him around the school, I thought, 'This is not the type of horse I like.' At that stage I did not appreciate that he simply couldn't get his body together to move it in a quick fashion. Everything he did was very ponderous, and as a result his training has been slow, but this is exactly what he needed.

He was uncomplicated to break and he was never 'backy' or temperamental, in fact, looking back, he was simply a large slug who constantly wanted human love. He is not the type, temperament or personality that I normally go for, but interestingly he has learned to be sharp. As a four-year-old he would hack out and never look at a thing, then suddenly on reaching six years old, after winning the National Championships where he spooked at everything, he has

Hector has very bendy hocks and, being a big horse, has not yet learned to swing through enough and push, so although we have activity and expression when he is ridden forward, at the moment it tends to tip him more onto his head.

become electric and very aware of his surroundings. It proves that big horses do take time to strengthen up.

Hector's strength kicked in when he was six years old and it has made him a very impressive horse. Now at eight I feel I am just beginning to turn the corner with him, but it has been a process of natural development with the emphasis on giving him time. As he grew up and strengthened, he filled out and became able to push, and this natural growth process, combined with simple exercises like transitions and pole and hill work, has helped him to develop. He was never forced to do endless movements in the school to build up his strength. So you can see that with some horses you have to know when to give them time to get their act together, and have the patience to wait for them to develop.

Training Advice

Contact Problems

In Hector's case, contact problems came from him not accepting the half-halt. He had a tendency to pull the rein down, and when asked to half-halt would lean on the hand and go overbent. At the same time he did not take the weight behind, as so often happens with contact problems.

The problem manifests itself in various ways: for example, if you have a very light-mouthed horse that is not taking the weight behind, it will overbend because it does not like the feeling of going against the bit. If, on the other hand, a horse is very strong and goes hollow because it does not take the weight behind, it will push out through the hand. So often contact problems stem from not accepting the half-halt. If a horse opens its mouth and resists because there is too much pressure from the rider, then the rider needs to go back to phase one of the half-halt and re-establish the 'stop/start' method again.

A rider can use the **rein back** to help with lightening the contact if the horse is too strong in the rein and the rider feels the half-halt is not working. The rein back sits the horse back, then the horse has to push forward and in doing so has to engage the hind legs without having the pressure in the front (this is because the backward-and-forward action of the rein back lightens the horse's forehand). The rein back certainly helps with horses that are getting very strong in the hand. It is best to do the exercise with a rider on board so the horse comes to understand the leg aids fully, too.

Hector is still very strong on the bit, and there is no doubt that this is linked to the fact that he is such a big mover. As a result of his movement he is thrusting forward against the hand a lot of the time, and in order to overcome this I ride him deeper than I would most horses. He might not look too bad, but I have to admit that he does not always feel so good as he is not submissive to the hand. To those watching he appears uphill, big-moving, soft and flowing, and he never changes his rhythm in all three paces, but I, as his rider, can feel that the contact is not right. A clever rider can disguise the problem, but at the end of the day the aim is to have a submissive, forward and obedient horse, so as the horse progresses the rider must look for ways to resolve the problem.

Contact plays a vital part in producing a true way of going; it cannot be fudged. Escapado's tension makes the contact irregular, and Hector has his problems, as I have just illustrated, so I, as a rider, must consult the scales of training and look for answers. There are a lot of horses competing at the higher levels of dressage these days, and the most important thing is that they do all the movements correctly and in balance. In other words, in balance and with self-carriage.

It takes time for big horses to find their balance and self-carriage, and a rider must allow for this if he wants to progress successfully to the next level. Greater collection is required of the horse as it progresses up the levels, so at Medium and Advanced Medium you would expect to see greater expression in the way the horse moves and a greater ease of movement.

The lateral movements come in at this level, both in trot and canter, including shoulder-in, travers and half-pass. These would all be expected in competition, and this is where your training to date is show-cased.

Is the horse even on both reins in half-pass and shoulder-in, and is he correctly bent? I always try to imagine, in the case of the bend, that the horse is really looking, with both eyes, where he is going. That is the amount of flexion required. At the same time, when performing shoulder-in or half-pass, he must maintain his bend and his rhythm. In addition the tempo must be regular and the horse must continue to swing.

Training Tip

Some horses, when they are learning to become more expressive, will gain more height, rhythm and expression on a straight line, but when they come to do half-pass the work is not as good and as a result they can be quite heavily penalised. So what can you do to improve that? I would try riding less acute angles combined with keeping the movement more forward.

Hector's contact problems stem from the fact that he is not yet strong enough in his hind legs. It is interesting because when you see him go from collected trot to extended trot he stays up, but when he goes from extended trot to collected trot he is not quick enough to bring his hind legs under. So the exercises to improve this are:

- Down the long side extended trot and transitions to halt at the far end.

- Extended trot down the long side then a transition to collected walk, maybe a half pirouette to engage the hind legs, then trot back.

- Transitions to walk doing waiting exercises so that the extension does not allow the horse to become too strong.

- The extensions at the moment need to be minimal so perhaps on half a long side extended trot, collect and then go again.

All the time I am looking for exercises to help Hector maintain his balance and increase the speed in his hind leg.

Travers

As previously mentioned, travers and half-pass are useful exercises for working on a horse's ability to bend around the rider's inside leg and engage his quarters. If leg-yielding and shoulder-in are established then a horse can move on to these exercises. They can encourage much more obedience to the rider's leg and rein aids. It is appropriate to look at this movement in greater depth at this stage since the rider is looking to reinforce these exercises to polish the horse's performance.

In travers, which is also known as quarters-in, the horse moves in the direction of the bend and his outside hind leg crosses over in front of his inside hind. The inside hind therefore bears more weight as the horse's body moves sideways and across.

Before you start lateral work of any kind, including travers, your aids must be fully accepted. The horse must be equally supple on both reins because problems such as uneven contact, or the horse not being forward enough, only get worse or more difficult when you start lateral work, which involves a higher degree of collection. If you have not done work of this kind before, it is a good idea to start in walk. This will give you a chance to co-ordinate the aids before moving on to trot and canter.

The best way to start travers is to ride the corner into the long side, then ride straight. The outside leg goes slightly behind the girth in a driving position and pushes the quarters into the school. The horse is then at an angle. The inside leg remains near the girth, where it can activate the inside hind leg. This together with an indication from the inside rein, is the way to achieve the correct bend. The outside rein secures the position of the horse's neck and the degree of bend. To achieve correct bend from the horse the rider must have a secure inside leg for creating activity.

To finish the travers at the end of the long side, straighten the horse before the corner. Allow plenty of time so that the horse is back on the track and totally straight before he negotiates the corner.

If the horse bends the neck too much, or brings the quarters in too much, it can affect the rhythm, and the hind leg will not carry enough weight as it will be pushed too much to the inside. To control the front, think of the front of the horse's face looking straight down the track and not to the inside.

Once the horse is supple it should be able to carry out all lateral movements fluently, moving from one to the other without changing the rhythm or outline. If the rider has difficulty with this, it is best to ask for less and stick to straightening the horse in between to achieve proper balance and confidence, rather than continuing when it is not right.

Canter Pirouettes

Walk Pirouette to Canter Pirouette

These can be ridden as 8–10-metre circles and are a way of re-establishing lightness when the canter pirouette becomes difficult. The rider can drop the horse back to a walk pirouette to show it the positioning again, and get him light to the leg aids through the walk.

It is important, particularly with younger horses, to employ exercises that do not always have the same degree of collection as the square exercise (see page 98). By this I mean use exercises which give the horse the idea of the movement but without any stress or great demands until the horse really understands what is required. Working on 20-metre and 10-metre circles does not demand so much collection; and indicating the bend and teaching the horse to maintain the three-beat canter are the most important aspects.

I also like to use exercises that help prevent anticipation, such as riding half a 10-metre circle in travers, then the other half in shoulder-in, then back to travers, and finally back to shoulder-in. In this way, not only are you suppling the horse the whole time, but also you are taking the initiative in how you want to ride the horse.

The importance of stretching. After the pressure of a movement such as a pirouette, it is important that the rider allows the neck muscles to move and stretch to maintain the softness in the back muscles and achieve a gymnastic top line. At the beginning of the session, sometimes the horse does not stretch fully, but by the end of the session he should have used his muscles more correctly so developing roundness in front of the saddle, as the photo shows.

Hector is picking up the new canter from the simple change, after the walk strides.

Simple Change

When a horse moves on to doing a simple change he is working towards being able to carry more weight behind in order to make an easy transition down. It is essential that the middle section of this movement, the walk, is correct.

Possible problems encountered are horses (particularly the young ones) anticipating the walk to canter.

■ Try riding canter to walk to shoulder-in in walk then cantering again. This not

This photo shows Hector preparing for the changes by doing canter-walk-canter, which is required at elementary level. Spencer has just asked Hector to walk, having made the canter to walk transition, and is waiting for the walk to be relaxed and achieve good rhythm before asking for the opposite canter lead.

only helps the horse to accept the rider's leg, but it also assists the rider because it encourages him to put his legs on the horse and not take the legs away at a time when the horse needs support. The exercise is good for horses that anticipate and for forward-going horses.

■ Another exercise would be to ride a turn around the forehand when you drop down to walk, so getting the horse to accept the leg, and again helping the rider to learn to keep the legs on and not take them away.

ABOVE: The turn across the school, using the quarter pirouette to transfer the weight back onto the hind leg. Hector makes an obedient transition.

LEFT AND BELOW: Good demonstration of picking up the new left canter and engagement.

A good illustration of the preparation for the turn for the simple change. Here the horse has been able to shift the weight back and use the turn in the school to help prepare for the movement. An excellent sequence.

Flying Changes

With a young horse never force the issue. If flying changes drive a horse mad, do them, then leave them for a week. Do not try to work on them every day. Go back to walk-canter-walk for a week before going back to the flying changes. A rider will create a problem with pressure and force.

If the horse continues to go crazy, then you might have to accept that it is not ready for changes.

Alternatively, if the horse does not respond to the leg at all, then it might benefit from working on the changes more often. This might make the horse a bit hotter, and so more responsive.

If a horse gets tense or starts to anticipate, then go back to basics before trying again.

In Hector's case he tends to get slow because his strides are so big, so we do medium canter down the long sides before the change and we ride the change in the same place we did the simple change so that he is not confused.

From Prix St Georges, where you have the changes every three or four strides, to Intermediaire I, where you have them every two strides, you should not have too many problems. In fact a lot of horses find it easier to change every two strides than every four because there are fewer strides in between for the horse to become crooked. The most important things that the judges are looking for are straightness and forwardness.

A lot of our training at home is spent practising the flying changes on the long sides, really using the walls; we seldom practise changing on the diagonals. In this way the horse never learns to become crooked, and he always gets a certain amount of security off the wall, so this is important. We also train our tempi changes on the wall before we would move to riding them on the diagonal line.

Medium Trot

The horse is learning to push more because he now has to become more elegant, more easy and more elevated, and obviously has to show some transitions between his working, collected and medium paces of the trot.

The horse should go evenly into both reins and remain straight in its body. The rider should carry his hands low and allow the horse to come through from behind into a longer outline. There should be swing in the horse's back so that the rider is carried smoothly with the forward movement. As the horse strengthens, the demands can be increased, but care needs to be taken in the early stages.

Hector is demonstrating the **medium trot**, and showing lightening of the shoulder and engagement of the hind leg.

Initially, Hector was not able to do medium trot, but after he had done **polework**, which got him stretching his whole body as he went over the poles, I was able to develop his trot.

RIGHT: I have set the poles on the ground. This is important for the horse's confidence and is an easy exercise.

BELOW RIGHT: More advanced polework, where I have lifted the poles onto supporting blocks. In this way the horse has to work a little harder through elevating the shoulder and pushing from the hind legs.

Medium Canter

For added expression in medium canter, the rider can place the shoulder slightly to the inside, in a shoulder-fore position, to develop the engagement of the inside hind leg. Remember: medium canter is about bigger strides **not** faster strides.

This is where horses with big paces, like Superman, can run into problems. It is very much easier for a horse with a small canter to make a transition down to walk from canter than it is for a horse with a big canter. A horse with a big canter may have to go a bit further in his training to learn more about collection. He is obviously more likely to be marked higher on his forward medium canters, because this is where he can show off, whereas a smaller-moving horse has to learn to go bigger.

I always say to my pupils, 'You have to look at what you have got and work with it!' Improvement comes with increasing the collection, which is the speed of the hind leg being able to come under the horse quicker, rather than the whole horse slowing down. Some riders think that because they have slowed their horse down it is then collected. This is not the case, but it is a trap that many fall into. The fact is that the hind legs have to work even harder and step under.

Here Hector shows a fantastic lift of the forehand – and the sky seems the limit!

Walk Pirouette

This movement involves the forehand of the horse making a half circle around the hind legs. The horse's inside hind leg should be raised and lowered with every step and not allowed to stand still (which is usually the major fault). Success depends on the degree of collection that the horse can achieve in the walk. Because it entails being able to move the hind leg quickly, horses blessed with a great big walk find it very difficult to move their hind leg at speed.

At elementary the horse is allowed to walk back in a diagonal line to the track if he finishes his turn away from it. That is the difference at the lower level compared to the more advanced level. The horse is not expected to turn around as if he is on a dinner plate, and I feel that a horse can understand a walk pirouette more easily after he has learned the walk half-pass.

A very good exercise that I teach my horses involves walking across a diagonal line in a half-pass and then making a full 360° circle at X in half-pass, which then becomes a walk pirouette. Bear in mind that in the training you teach the horse to half-pass around his circle, and when you get to the walk pirouette you are just teaching the horse to turn his front around his hind legs – but he has learned through the half-pass to stay off the outside leg, and so avoids falling prey to that often seen fault where the horse steps out against the rider's leg. The horse must understand that the outside leg controls the quarters.

Shoulder-In

The aim of this exercise is to achieve a higher degree of collection, balance and lightness, which in turn will improve straightness. Through bending and going straight the horse becomes more supple and takes more weight on the inside hind leg. All three major hind-leg joints are exercised, so suppleness and activity produce more freedom of the horse's shoulder.

Reminders for Shoulder-In

- Always look for the outside foreleg to come down on the inside of the track

- If you can see the corner of the horse's eye and the corner of his mouth on the inside, this is enough bend

- When riding tests, the tempo and length of stride should be the same, and the angle should be symmetrical on both reins

- Make the corner work for you and use it in the preparation of the movement

Shoulder-in on a circle

This is also ideal for young horses as the horse is already bent round the inside leg. On the circle indicate the direction inwards with the inside rein. The outside rein stops the horse bending too much to the inside and stops the outside shoulder falling out. The inside leg maintains the bend and encourages the inside hind leg to step well under the horse's body as well as maintaining the forward movement. The rider's outside leg supports to stop the hindquarters falling out. In lateral work the rider must maintain the same quality, forward, rhythmic trot as on the straight.

Shoulder-in down the long side

This exercise is easiest either when coming out of the corner or a 10-metre circle, as you can use the bend you already have and continue the movement up the track. Do not do the whole length to start with, concentrate on a few good steps. If the horse stiffens, turn him into a 10-metre circle to establish the bend and the rhythm again. Keep using the 10-metre circle up the long side, but don't keep going with the shoulder-in, in the hope that it will come right, if all momentum is lost. Make sure that there is a start and a finish to the exercise, and when coming out of the shoulder-in be careful to straighten your horse.

More Advanced Shoulder-In

For more established horses ride a 20-metre circle, say left, in shoulder-in right, decreasing the circle to about 10 metres. Bring the horse's front end round to the inside, changing to shoulder-in left, and gradually increase the circle back out to 20 metres. This exercise encourages greater activity and suppleness on both reins without having to change rein. The rider's weight must be shifted onto the inside seat bone – just push down a little more into your inside stirrup. Do not allow your weight to slide to the outside, which then collapses the inside hip. Look up in the direction you are going.

With the shoulder-in, some prefer three tracks and others four. Neither is incorrect providing the horse is doing the same thing on both reins and the angle is equal on both reins. The engagement of the hind leg is the most important aspect of shoulder-in, and the bend should involve the whole body. Neck bend alone is not shoulder-in.

The most common fault is the horse falling out through the outside shoulder. This is usually because the rider is using too much inside rein to get the bend and not enough inside leg to support it, or he is failing to maintain the contact on the outside rein.

A horse that finds it more difficult to accept the outside rein is more likely to fall out through the outside shoulder. To correct this, have a stronger contact with the outside rein to give more support while asking for less bend. Most horses are more hollow to the right, so the shoulder-in on the right rein is not as easy to perfect. If the pace drops and the steps shorten, or if impulsion is lost, then straighten the horse and ride forwards to refresh the pace before trying again.

Medium tests

Choose your medium tests carefully. Some are more difficult than others and should only be attempted after successfully establishing the horse at medium through the other less-demanding tests.

Chapter Eight

Training the Nine- and Ten-Year-Olds

Prix St Georges/Intermediaire is a big step up for a horse as the movements are more demanding. Horses working at this level should be able to show a greater degree of gymnastic ability reflected in the expression of their movements. In this chapter Dolendo is shown carrying out some of these movements and it is perhaps a testimony to my entire team's patience and understanding that he has made it to this level at all, since he was an extremely difficult youngster. He does illustrate how patience and lateral thinking in a horse's training can make all the difference as to whether or not the horse becomes a champion.

DOLENDO (10 years)

Dolendo, or Donald to his friends, is by Donnerhall and came from Gronwohldhof, the same stud and training centre as his famous sire. Bought unseen, on the recommendation of Sandy Phillips, he was known to be naughty, but many years of patient training are now reaping the rewards. He was undoubtedly a horse with a difficult temperament – in his early days he had the ability to win one day, then get thrown out of the ring the next for failing to behave. He has now reached 'small tour', where he will stay for a while to consolidate what he has learned, because of his personality and also his size. Donald and Hector are alike for two reasons: first, they are both huge; and second, they were all I could afford at the time.

FACING PAGE: Dolendo in his early days, showing his potential.

When I bought Donald I knew that he could be difficult but he wasn't expensive so, although buying him was a risk, it would not have been the end of the world if it hadn't worked out. In truth, he was not rideable at all, so I sent him away to get rid of his nappiness. He just did not want to be ridden. He looked magnificent but I knew there had been some breaking problems. There was not a lot of difficulty in getting on him, it was just everything else! He didn't actually try to get you off; he was just very nappy, and, of course, huge with it. Because he was so enormous he had problems getting round corners and doing turns, and he had really wonky legs in those days – big baby legs which went everywhere. He also has pigeon toes, and although condemned by a judge in a young horse class for the two big splints on his front legs, to this day he remains a very sound horse. When he was younger, though, he could not do too much work because of his legs, which made life difficult because he was so naughty and really needed to work. Despite his ups and downs, and having some time out when he was hobdayed, Donald has gone from strength to strength, but with his size and personality he does take a lot of riding.

■ Exercises

Collected and Extended Walk

The walk has a four-time beat; a horse should walk with purpose and make the four-beat sequence clear to the observer. Each foot must be picked up actively and put down firmly and squarely. Lack of impulsion will prevent this clear picture and the feet will, more often than not, be dragged.

A horse should go forward and it is important that the rider learns the natural

Donald showing a particularly good example of **extended walk**.

length of the horse's stride so that the controlling aids can be applied without destroying the natural steps.

Collected walk comes from the development of engagement of the hindquarters and greater submission to the aids. The steps will be shorter than the natural steps and the hind feet will not overtrack, but there should be no restriction or loss of the four-beat sequence.

Extended walk is closer to the natural stride but, due to increased impulsion, it covers more ground. It is important for the neck to nod out more in order to get the full length in the top line. The rider rides the extension with his hands and hips.

Rein Back

This is a test of obedience, and this is why it is included in the tests. The horse obviously has to remain diagonal and in rhythm. Two common faults are: the horse pulling against the rider's hand, and the rider dragging the horse back with his hands. The results of this are that the horse loses its diagonal step or drags its feet or both.

There are several ways to correct this. First, lighten your seat when you rein back and brace a little against the reins. Also, bring the lower leg slightly back, lightening your seat and every time (in the beginning) the horse steps back, let go of the reins. Each time they take a step let go, stop, then take another step, stop and let go, so that the horse eventually, with the slightest touch of the rein together with the leg aid, steps back.

If you are still stuck and the horse will not do it correctly, you can try the movement from the ground without a rider on the horse's back. If the horse is very crooked, put a pole on the floor and rein back between the pole and the wall or side. A lot of young horses do go crookedly, and you see riders trying to correct the crookedness by pushing the quarters back. In fact the easiest way is to correct the shoulders. If the horse is reining back and he goes quarters to the left, do not use more left leg and correct him like that. Instead, turn the front end to the left and rein him back with the front to the left, because pushing so much with the leg will only create more problems.

Transitions in and out of rein back should be fluid and effortless. Remembering that the rein-back movement requires a great deal of throughness and collection. It should not be the long, flat movement that is so often seen.

The rein-back sequence in Intermediaire I is four steps back, four steps forward and four steps back, so you are looking for diagonal (two-beat) steps back, a four-beat rhythm forward and then diagonal steps back again. It is important to have lightness in your hand. Being able to rein your horse back with an invisible aid and a lightness in your hand is all-important. This enables the horse to be able to carry itself lightly backwards and not lean against the hand, which often makes it push its neck out against the bit and drop its back, giving you the feeling that the middle of the back has sunk and the hind legs have gone. It is a question of training the horse to respond to a soft aid.

Working from the ground, with a rider on the back to help the horse, with

Training Tip

Lightening the seat in rein back is important. This is particularly so with young horses because when they go back they arch their backs, creating tightness and stiffness from the arching. You do not want to be pushing down at the very moment they need the load to be lightened a little to enable them to move back.

Reining back, with a light seat.

someone holding a stick in front of the horse and just moving him back with a hand placed on his shoulder, is another very good exercise. The horse will learn that when a rider touches him he should move back, and the person on the ground will reinforce the aid and give the horse the confidence to do it. It is a particularly good way to teach rein back if you meet resistance from the horse, and some horses do get nervous about going backwards. They either run backwards or they resist, so rein back is something that needs to be handled with care.

Canter Pirouettes

Donald has needed to spend a lot of time doing canter-walk-canter to improve his collection in the canter. He was tending to shorten the stride rather than engage it; he did not stay under with his hind leg and would make small bunny hops behind. Donald's size and weight play an important part. We had to be careful not to force the issue of pirouettes as he needed big working pirouettes to gain confidence to keep a clear three-beat rhythm. All the time we were using exercises to make him stronger. Essentially we allowed him the freedom to do slightly bigger pirouettes

Donald is learning to take the weight behind, and half pirouettes help the learning process, as well as being required in Prix St Georges.

The first thing you have to think about in the half pirouette is bringing the horse back onto his hind leg and then turning the front around the back end, not pushing the hind legs in. In this photo Donald has his hind leg underneath his stomach and he is going to turn his front end around his hind leg, not jump to the inside, which is a fault you often see.

Training Tip

A good exercise for horses who 'take over' in pirouettes, is to leg-yield them into the pirouette. If riding right canter then leg-yield two to three strides to the left and then make the pirouette so they learn to stay upright and not lean in.

than are stipulated at this level, because that's what he needed.

Canter pirouettes on the centre line are extremely difficult because the judge requires the horse to be absolutely straight before the pirouette. To work on this use a leg-yielding exercise. Come down on the right rein, for example, and slightly leg-yield the horse to the left before you turn, and this will help supple the horse and bend him. This is an exercise for an advanced horse. What we are trying to do is create the activity **before** the pirouette rather than upset him and make the activity **in** the pirouette. This way he has heightened energy before the pirouette then relaxation as he turns.

RIGHT: Leg-yielding before the pirouette.

FAR RIGHT: The horse flexing around the rider's inside leg. This is good preparation for teaching the horse to canter in a straight line, particularly up and down the centre line just with these flexions, without ever anticipating turns.

Very good pirouette sequence.

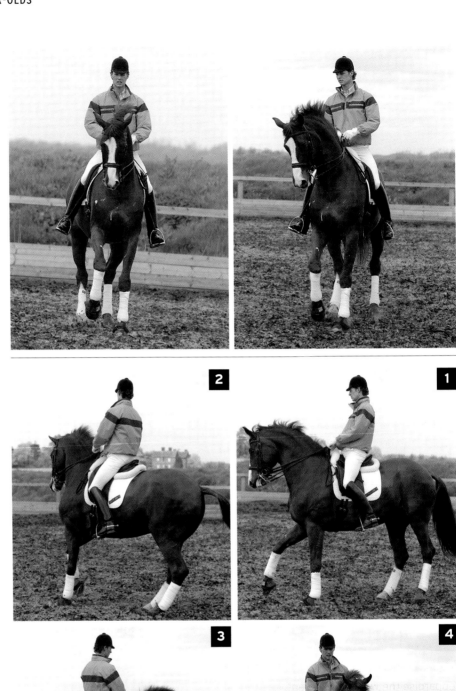

Zig-Zag Half-Pass

In Prix St Georges this tends to be ridden to the centre line, then change, and back. In Intermediaire I the zig-zag is four strides, then two of eight strides, then four again. What is being looked for is that the rhythm of the canter can be maintained, so the rider has to make sure the horse is equally bent, and the flying changes are straight; the rider must not allow the horse to change sideways. There are exercises which can be done to help this.

Exercises to improve the zig-zag

The best exercise for the zig-zag is to ride the horse sideways in a half-pass, and change the bend into a leg-yield so he doesn't always anticipate that when you change the bend you are going in a new direction and he learns to stay off your outside leg. You can then change straight, ride half-pass the other way, and then turn that into a leg-yield before riding straight again and making the change. If you hesitate with your aids then it is very easy to lose the stride and jeopardise the whole movement.

Practise the zig-zag from the long side – it is more relaxing for the horse because it can use the wall for security, and you, as the rider, can be more sure about the crossing over. The steps should be equal to the left and to the right: for example, eight strides off and eight strides back, making sure that the half-pass steps are very measured.

Another exercise is to do half-pass to the left and then ride either a leg-yield or shoulder-in so that the horse does not anticipate before you ask for the change because very often they will slip in the change. Make the horse wait by doing a shoulder-in in the new direction and make him wait three or four steps before the change.

Very good canter pirouette sequence showing more jump and illustrating how the weight is carried on the hind legs.

When riding zig-zags, remember: if you hesitate with your aids then it is very easy to lose the stride and jeopardise the whole movement.

Piaffe and Passage

Donald is still on a learning curve as far as these two movements are concerned. To begin with, he just does half steps to get the back to come up and really swing. For a young horse without the necessary strength, this makes the work much less demanding, because with half steps he does not have to take so much weight on his hind legs, he just establishes the rhythm. As the session goes on, Donald is encouraged to carry more weight behind.

Donald is such a big horse that he has found passage difficult. Pushing work (which is what passage is all about) is hard for him and he could not trot slowly enough and stay engaged. If he slowed he would disengage, but by using lots of rising trot to encourage him to keep using his back in the collection, he has just learned passage. In learning to produce the elevation we have now, as he has got stronger, he has also developed the ability to go forward more into expressive collection. Passage is a very good way of teaching a horse to become expressive in its trot. After only three weeks training he is already looking good.

Donald is being allowed to stretch in the piaffe for his relaxation. The stretching of the top line in piaffe encourages him to be soft in his back, and this is very much a training piaffe to encourage the swing. With the horse stretched so much, he does not have to carry the weight behind; it is more a question of getting a fairly horizontal balance.

Here we are teaching Donald to stay stretched and go very forward in his piaffe and start to really climb forward in the movement. When this photo was taken he was just below Grand Prix level; he has yet to learn about transitions in this movement. So I make him piaffe on the spot then go forward then piaffe again, and so on, so he starts to learn about the transitions.

He is now taking the weight behind and lowering his joints but softly, without jarring.

ABOVE: We are encouraging Donald's trot to have more cadence and expression, via the suspension of passage. You have to be careful not to get the trot too like passage, but when training, this exercise teaches rhythm and encourages the horse to stay carrying the weight. It is a process of going forward then back again, then forward again, until the horse starts to get lightness and elegance in his trot.

RIGHT: Donald is starting to develop this new trot.

Training Tip

Most horses can be taught to trot more expressively as trot is the easiest pace to change. Donald's trot has progressed from flat to expressive by use of the passage.

After a lot of collected work it is a good idea to ride some extensions to get the elasticity and impulsion through the forward movement again. Notice how much more lift and height he gets through his shoulder. This 'on and back' technique gives him the strength to develop his new 'show' trot, which he really does with expression.

Chapter Nine

Training the Grand Prix Horse

Once the horse has mastered piaffe and passage, the rider can feel satisfied that the horse's training is complete, as by now the horse should be capable of all the movements of the Grand Prix, which is the ultimate goal in dressage riding.

The training must aim for the horse to be supple in the movements, not just able to do them. The horse needs rhythm, swing and elevation, with the rider appearing to be doing nothing. This comes from the refinement of the aids and the suppleness of the horse. It takes years of patient training to reach this level, and by this stage the horse should trust his rider and the rider should be able to communicate with his horse with completely harmonious aids. This is what I am aiming for with Escapado.

ESCAPADO (11 years)

Escapado (aka Peanuts) is by the Thoroughbred stallion Ex Libris. He is very Thoroughbred-like and has always reverted to the 'flight' mechanism when challenged. In the early days whenever things went wrong he would panic and fly, which did not make him the easiest of horses. Today he is more settled, but as a youngster he proved a real challenge.

He was originally found by Michel and Mette Assouline in Germany at the Oldenburg auctions in Vechta, in 1996, when he was three years old. They both felt Peanuts was just the horse for me, and when I saw him it was love at first

Escapado in his first Grand Prix at the tender age of ten. The expression on his face shows he is listening to me.

sight. However, the early days proved very exciting. Peanuts, a hot horse at the best of times, used to take off regularly in the outdoor school, which at that time was situated right by the road where the traffic thundered past and the lorries tested their air-brakes with extraordinary frequency. It is a blessing that he is so good in the stable, where he is exceptionally kind and loving.

In the early days I think I demanded too much of him – I expected a lot because I knew he was extremely talented. I felt frustrated and could not understand why he couldn't (or wouldn't) do what I wanted. Spencer used to ride him a bit, and a German girl who was working for me used to do walk, trot and canter on him for 45 minutes each day. Having less-demanding riders on him for over 50 per cent of the time, allowed him to work out what we were asking. Fortunately we had time on our side. You cannot, after all, manufacture Grand Prix horses; sometimes you have to change tactics and let things 'cook' more slowly.

His turnaround came when we moved to our current yard and I let him live out. He was out at grass all the time initially, day and night, and he suddenly became very chilled out. He found the work very easy and overcame his mental blocks. He was seven then, and he realised that he could relax for 23 hours of the day. He was being ridden for only one hour and the rest of the time he was living in the field. Just like Pro Set who needed to be ridden first in a 'peace' hour, so living out in the field got Peanuts through his barrier. After that it was easy to do the work; and he became obedient because he was accepting the work and wasn't so tense. This enabled us to move on to the next stage of submissiveness.

Peanuts is so relaxed nowadays that he finds the work much easier. As a result, I am able to incorporate some more difficult work into his routine, like changes round circles. This type of movement is more than is required at Grand Prix, so when he does compete at that level it should almost be a little bit easy for him. He will start to go to more and more shows, both at home and abroad, so that he will get into the competition rhythm, and things such as going on the lorry become more routine. The more familiar it all becomes, the more we can start to create the same work at shows that we can do at home.

At home I am still working on the contact. The key to riding Peanuts is to have the right contact. He likes to be a little bit running into the hand because he is very forward going. At home, now that we have established the relaxation, I can get him very light – and he feels fantastic when he is light – so I am working on trying to improve this, especially in the walk and canter.

When it comes to competitions Peanuts is definitely an 'outdoor' horse rather than an 'indoor' one. Distractions are far greater indoors, with the public almost on top of the arenas, and the noise is too great. Indoors he can get very worked up, to the point that I can feel his heart beating and he only relaxes if I keep chattering quietly to him through the test. Communication makes a big difference to him. With Peanuts it is a question of producing the goods on the day consistently – his talent has never been in any doubt.

FACING PAGE: Total concentration for both horse and rider.

Training Advice

Canter Half-Pass

Having established travers in canter, you should be ready to move to the half-pass. The canter half-pass must remain fresh and in a good three-beat rhythm. If your trot half-pass is established with good rhythm and bend, you can be sure that you are doing everything correctly. Often canter half-pass can be easier because the co-ordination of the aids is already there, but if it is not correctly established it can lead to the three-time rhythm breaking up because the rider is only concentrating on going sideways and not on the quality of the pace.

Two tips for testing riding are:

- Always imagine starting half-pass with a step of shoulder-in first, to stop the horse coming through the corner and starting off with his quarters leading.

- Bring your inside shoulder and inside hip back slightly to give a better impression of you moving with your horse in the direction you are travelling and not against it.

Escapado demonstrating his gymnastic ability with good flexion through the entire body.

Canter Pirouettes

A rider needs to establish a training programme for each horse. It depends on how mature and established a horse is as to which exercises you work on. Younger horses might do walk pirouettes to canter pirouettes, while an established Grand Prix horse can practise the exercise within a square created by jump poles (see photo on page 98). This latter exercise is extremely hard work and a younger, less established horse would not be ready to attempt it. Peanuts would have no problem, whereas Donald might find it more difficult.

Another way to train canter pirouettes is by working a canter half-pass, riding a big circle then canter half-pass again. If tension sets in, go back to basics until the horse is relaxed before trying the exercise once again – this applies to any exercise you try.

Half-Pirouettes

A correct half-pirouette in a test would be seen to have three or four strides, in as small a half circle around the haunches as possible. The most difficult part is sustaining the tempo of the canter with the horse flexed and bent in the direction in which it is moving; the degree of collection that is necessary shows that the horse is able to carry the weight behind.

Judges will be looking for a straight line in, a well-executed pirouette, and a straight line out.

Problems at this level are very much down to riders pushing the horse sideways in a half-pass as they come to their pirouette. Because they want their horse to turn, the first thing they do is push the horse to the inside so that the horse makes a half-pass step (or two) and then executes the pirouette. By this stage the horse has made a very large half circle – and this is something that really needs to be seen because it is very difficult to feel while you are turning in the pirouette. Riders often miss the fact that they have moved their horse to the side in the beginning. So it makes sense to learn to ride the shoulder-fore position or shoulder-in angles before you make these pirouettes.

The thing a rider should think about when turning in a pirouette is the front end, not the back end. A very good way to remember this is the phrase 'start tight and get bigger', rather than start big and get tighter because obviously you need more impulsion on the way out – well actually you need as much impulsion on the way in as on the way out, but usually impulsion is lost on the way out and this is where a problem develops.

Canter pirouettes, be they half pirouettes or full pirouettes, should never really be practised as part of a test rehearsal at home because they are something that a horse very easily learns to anticipate. Riding squares with quarter pirouettes in each corner can be more beneficial. This exercise has a two-fold benefit in that the horse is given a break in between each turn, just to relax his stride before he re-collects and does another turn, and it prevents the horse from anticipating. If the exercise is moved around the school and is never performed in one place, this also helps.

Something else that is useful when riding the pirouette is to 'feel' a stride of leg-yield before you pirouette, so you almost push the horse away from the way he is going to turn. What this does is give you the chance to bring the horse up on your inside leg so that he is upright for his turn and not turning against the leg.

Pirouette Exercises on a Square – for advanced horses and those at Grand Prix

This is a highly collected movement within a square, and it is something that can help you, as the rider, to get the right feel and the ultimate control over the horse, depending of course on what size square you use. You can set up your square in the school, using jump poles on the ground. If the square is approximately 8 x 8 metres, the exercise is quite a challenge. It is amazing how confined a square feels, and to canter pirouette your horse round you really need to use the corners to get the positioning right, as the horse has to turn at that precise moment.

When riding the square, you don't have the luxury of the preparation that you would normally have in your schooling. For example, when schooling, you can wait till everything feels perfect before doing the movement, whereas on the square you have to turn or you sail out over a pole.

The exercise is obviously for a horse which is very developed in his collection and able to maintain the weight. It is important to remember that all the movements should flow.

With Peanuts, who is a very intelligent horse, I had to deal with a common problem for such horses. As soon as he learned the pirouette, he liked to turn without me, especially in tests, leaving me with a G-force face because he had gone round so fast.

Also the pirouettes never really came right in a test situation, until he was ten

Square exercise with poles. Escapado demonstrates the need for high collection and concentration to ride this precise movement of canter pirouettes within a confined space.

Half a pirouette of walk, followed by a canter stride of pirouette, then back to walk pirouette. This exercise is to accustom the horse to wait for the rider's aids.

years old, partly because he liked to take over, and partly because any tension in him always came out in the canter. He used to get both hind legs going together because he would stiffen his back, rather than just lower and let go and turn on his inside hind leg. This was changed by teaching him to stretch in a pirouette so he was not able to get so short and tight. He had to have plenty of work with a much looser rein and a longer frame, so encouraging his back to stay very rounded and his neck down. He had to learn to step under with length in his top line, so I worked him on a 20-metre circle to encourage him to really canter on and build up impulsion, then rode a 10-metre circle. I had to see that he still had a very stretched neck on the smaller circle, to encourage him to remain through behind, and not automatically over-collect and over-shorten. I had to give and re-take the reins in the pirouette, and get him to follow my hand down so he couldn't shorten his frame so much, which enabled him to get very strong in a stiff, wrong way.

The Full Pirouette

A correct full pirouette should be between six and eight strides. Many horses slow down and elevate too much, which shows that they have lost the impulsion, and they tend to turn in four or five strides. This is incorrect but following some of the exercises already explained, a rider can prevent this problem.

One-Tempi Changes

In Intermediaire II a rider has only to perform eleven one-times, whereas in Grand Prix it is fifteen. Some horses learn these much more easily than others, depending on the type of canter they possess. They have to be balanced enough to trust that they can really do this.

The horse has to be very confident in its two-tempi changes before trying for one-times. A very good way of learning the one-tempi changes is to get the horse to do just two one-tempi changes. You need to be able to achieve this on both reins before you start to string them together. The rider will teach a horse left-right on one rein, and right-left on the other rein. This is really where you start to appreciate how well the horse is working from your aids and whether he understands the sequence of the legs and how the flying change works. I would teach this on the long sides, where the horse has the wall to help keep him straight.

One thing to remember when you are teaching flying changes: do not over-correct the horse when it makes a mistake. If you do, you will be repaid later on when you see that when they make a mistake they get nervous or hot. This is possibly a sign that they are not established enough in the work. You need trust between horse and rider if you are to consolidate the one-time changes.

Try not to think about the horse when you are doing the one-time changes, think instead about your aids. The horse needs to fit in with your aids, because they either slow down in the movement or they speed up, and you must keep your aids consistent. The horse must fit in with you to learn them. All riders put their own rhythm into horses, so much so it is often possible to see who has trained which horse, or who has ridden a particular horse.

One-time changes are a very rhythmical exercise, and they can be very easy to train. Sometimes, riding in a big, open space really helps a horse. A line of two-tempi changes going into one-tempi changes is a very good way of picking up the confidence and the rhythm.

Some horses that are hesitant in the changes need to be ridden very forward for a couple of long sides in medium canter to add impulsion to the pace. Try riding two one-tempi changes (i.e. left and right) at the beginning of the long side, then ride forward in medium canter and do two one-tempi changes at the other end of the long side. Before you string more one-tempi changes together, this forward way of riding needs to be established.

The aim is to have the schooling so good that the rider has very light, quiet, subtle aids, though inevitably during the teaching, the rider's aids, particularly the leg, will be emphasised.

Piaffe and Passage

Not every horse has the capability to do piaffe and passage, which is why there are so few horses at Grand Prix level. It is often not just a matter of conformation, or the way the horse is built, or indeed the fact that he has not been trained properly. Some horses do not have the quality, which limits their ability. They lack the eagerness to go forward or the temperament to cope. There are a lot of horses that are not big movers, but they have wonderful piaffe and passage because they have a natural ability to sit and spring, but usually they are horses that want to go. Basically it is in them!

If you get to the point where your horse is not able to do it, and does not offer it, you have to accept that horses have their limitations. There have been horses that have won internationally at Small Tour level but that have not moved up to the Grand Prix circuit because they did not have piaffe and passage in them.

Earlier I talked about watching young horses to see if they give an indication of what they can do naturally, when they get nervous or excited. There are various

> Remember that piaffe and passage are just trot – albeit that piaffe is a lowered trot on the spot, while passage is a trot with high elevation.

Escapado showing an expressive **piaffe**. Note the flexion in all the joints behind. This is why it is incredibly important to have built up the carrying power to achieve this collection.

ways of discovering if a horse can piaffe and passage: in-hand, from the back, or on long reins, as I have discovered with the various horses that are in this book.

Peanuts is a natural piaffe and passage horse, while Donald is a better at piaffe than he is at passage, so we have to teach him that. Pro Set and Groove Jet both show a little bit of both: Pro Set shows it when he gets excited, while Groove Jet shows it when tapped on the hindquarters. Superman, when touched on the rump, shows that he can do it, and you can see that it is there.

Passage can be learned on the long reins. I don't have the reins running along the horse's sides as is normally seen but instead have them running through a loop on the top of the saddle. To me, this is more like being 'ridden' from the ground than being 'driven' from the ground. It gets the horse more in tune with the rider, and it is obviously easier without a rider on their back. It is just a matter of giving them a helping hand.

When schooling these movements at home it is important to do some of the work with a 'light seat in rising trot'. This applies to the piaffe but particularly, the passage. The rising trot is really good in helping the horse gain the height. If you push into your heel it can really help the horse in the rising to come off the floor. It frees up the back and you can 'bring the horse up with you' when you rise, which is

Escapado, at an early stage, demonstrating **passage**. Ideally he could show more lift of the foreleg, but this is rhythmic and in balance.

why it is so useful. It also helps you to be lighter on the horse's back.

Piaffe and passage are both forms of elevated trot, so if you can gain height then so much the better. It can feel strange to rise, but it can often give the horse rhythm. You must, however, have good balance and an established seat to do this correctly. You need to be able to ride without drawing back on the reins to bring the horse into the movement, and without using the reins to try to find balance. In other words, you need to be experienced with a good independent seat to do it.

Escapado, having just won the final Grand Prix of the 2004 Spanish tour - and we are united in delight.

Chapter Ten

Other Horses – Other Techniques

SANTAS

Santas appears, on the surface, to be an easy horse who is naturally talented. He is without doubt a professor in his abilities to understand all he is taught, and he is such a laid-back character he could be considered a dream ride. However, he does have a problem in that he needs to be motivated. When it comes to competitions he definitely lacks the 'killer instinct' and this is far more difficult to resolve than it might initially appear.

His reliability means he only takes some ten to fifteen minutes of stretching to work in, which puts him at the other end of the spectrum entirely from Peanuts. However, we have now found that what he needs is a little positive tension in his work at home and before he goes into a test. This is so that he gives a little more in the arena than he has previously been used to, and although it might sound a straightforward procedure it has, in fact, taken over a year of hard work before it has finally started to pay off.

He has three good paces, including an exceptional canter, as well as being straight and 100 per cent reliable in any conditions. His philosophy seems to be, 'the quicker I do my working in, the quicker I do my test and the quicker I can get back to my stable'. As a result of his laid-back approach he never really worked hard, and so was never properly fit.

I am now much more awake to the fact that this type of horse needs to be got really fit, with a lot of hill work and cantering on gallops, in a similar way to an eventer. It is important for their lungs as well as their general stamina, since once a horse is at an advanced level it may well spend ten to fifteen minutes working on a particular exercise in canter.

Riding a horse like this makes its demands on the rider too. The horse needs to be lifted out of a rut and made to work just a little more energetically than he would normally. It should be stressed that this must not be hurried so the horse loses his balance, but he has to be worked just fractionally out of his comfort zone with a little more activity. We hope that the horse will get accustomed to this (new) way of going and so produce greater activity and energy in his work. In turn, this should give his performance a great deal more sparkle and make him a winner rather than just being in the places.

DONNER RHAPSODY (MADONNA)

Madonna is a full sister to Grand Prix stallion, Donnersong, both of whom were bred by Kate Carter. She is a very intelligent horse but being a mare needs a little bit more 'kid-glove' treatment. She was, I came to the conclusion, a horse that felt confined in arenas, particularly those indoors, so I chose to work her in the field, as it gave her a feeling of freedom and open spaces, which undoubtedly suited her temperament and character. Springy turf is much more to her liking, and once we made this change in her training regime she became much more relaxed and responsive in her work. We also turned her out in the paddock for some time each day.

Madonna has as a natural aptitude for piaffe and passage but she just needed the energy which came from being ridden outside. She was a backwards-thinking horse in the school, and was always looking at things, which was the reason I believe that she felt confined. Her reticence showed

Madonna feeling the freedom of the great outdoors.

Although Madonna is out in the middle of a field, she still relaxes to do the stretching work.

particularly in her changes and they used to get shorter and shorter. By riding her a lot in the field, where you could take a line across two acres and do medium canter, a few changes then medium canter again, the whole thing suddenly became enjoyable to her.

Madonna is one of the few mares that I have trained and, having done so, conclude that you do need to be a bit more compromising with mares. The message was not getting through to her in the school. Pushing her more in the

Madonna showing enhanced collection as the open space has given her energy.

school just made her more tense, but this did not happen in the field. She really came on in leaps and bounds and found her one-tempi changes, piaffe and passage very easy once I started working on grass. She was fantastic and got incredible height out there.

She is now with Annie MacDonald-Hall on the Grand Prix circuit.

OTHER TECHNIQUES

The Pen and Turning Out

Although top dressage horses are valuable commodities these days, all my horses get turned out, and are hacked out, and I find it not only relaxes them but it helps to keep their legs in good order. I believe it is vital for every horse to be turned out each day, irrespective of sex, type or age. Horses should go out even in winter, and this is when a pen is very useful. It prevents fields from being wrecked but allows the horses the opportunity to have a buck and kick and get rid of any frustrations. None of my horses are in their stables 23 hours a day, and they all take other forms of exercise besides their training. This is essential for their minds and also good for their joints (through the movement).

In summer they can all go out for longer, and even Peanuts, although working at Grand Prix level, goes out for a few hours each day. Being turned out changed his life – as a result of him living out all the time he became

Escapado enjoying a well-earned break.

Hector seeing the funny side of life.

rideable and more accepting of the rider. Now it is very good for his relaxation, and, although he does not have to go out and he is no longer unrideable, it is better all round for his quality of life.

Hacking

If you can do it, take your horse hacking, and if possible do some hill work. Riding up hills improves wind fitness as well as muscular fitness. When you are schooling and working on a canter movement, it's easy to find yourself cantering for at least ten minutes. That requires a lot of wind fitness from the horse. Stamina is required if the horse is to breathe and work for this period of time, so having good lung capacity is very important.

Hector often finishes his work by going for a 7-furlong gallop, which he thoroughly enjoys, and usually ends up pulling like a bull. What is interesting about the 'warmblood' types' is that they often don't know how to gallop. Once Hector cottoned on, he really took hold and let rip. These horses learn it quickly and it brightens them up no end.

Santas was really helped by doing fast work because he was a stuffy type, and for those that do not have to be worked so much it is a wonderful way to let off steam and energy.

Fitness

The importance of fitness should not be underestimated, and riders need to remember that not all horses get fit in the school. When riding at Grand Prix level a horse needs to be tight (muscled up) and fit to take the schooling,

Madonna appreciated a good gallop and a change of scenery. Dexter, my dog, tries to keep up.

whatever its age, shape and size.

Some horses are definitely easier to keep fit than others. Peanuts is the type of horse who would get fit simply by walking because everything he does is energetic. However, for most other horses Peanuts' work regime would certainly not be enough, so cantering the horse and really concentrating on wind fitness is essential.

Chapter Eleven

The Team

The team that supports me on a day-to-day basis, as well as before and after competitions, is vital for ensuring that the horses are in tip top condition at all times. The whole philosophy is one of prevention rather than cure, so all the horses are regularly checked by both the vet and the physiotherapist, and the farrier visits every few weeks to ensure no problems could potentially be building up. By supervision from these experts, combined with skilful daily monitoring by my groom Caroline Dawson, I aim to nip problems in the bud before any injury or illness becomes chronic.

THE VET - Buffy Shirley-Beavan

Buffy has been involved with high-level sports horses for a number of years, and works on three major, straightforward principles: firstly, the horse must be healthy; secondly, it must be comfortable in its back; and thirdly, it needs to be sound. A dressage horse is no different from any other top performance horse, although soundness has to be 110 per cent because the horse is under such scrutiny in its paces, and it must be comfortable in its back. It is therefore useful to have a good physiotherapist involved, like Maggie Turner (see page 114) who works with Buffy on my horses.

If Buffy looks at the whole horse and finds some pain in the neck or back, she will look for lameness problems elsewhere which she will treat accordingly. It may be that the horse requires some form of manual therapy from Maggie, and if the problem still exists then Maggie will refer it back to Buffy. So Buffy and Maggie's work is very much a two-way process. If there is a mechanical problem within the back there may still be pain whether Buffy treats it or 'shock-waves' it – using a type of pressure-wave treatment that is very good for easing back pain and promoting healing – so then she will need Maggie's expertise to help get it right, otherwise it is only a temporary solution. Maggie leaves Buffy notes or, if the case is complicated, she will call Buffy to discuss the

(From left to right) Peanuts, Buffy and Maggie.

various issues. Both Maggie and Buffy will trot horses up to get a better picture of the problem, and as a great deal of lameness and back problems are inter-related it is important to treat both ends of the spectrum to get the problem corrected.

The riders here are very much part of this teamwork, as we can give the vet and the physiotherapist valuable feedback to enable a diagnosis to be made. We know when a horse is not working properly, when it has lost performance, when it should be working better or simply that it is lame.

Treatments have really advanced over the years, with improved forms of joint medication, and keyhole surgery, which allows safe and effective removal of chips from joints in young horses. If the vet can treat a joint problem, and the physio can treat the back problem that has occurred as a result, and the farrier can then deal with the consequential foot imbalance, it is quite possible that the vet will not have to re-treat the joint. Once the horse starts using itself normally, everything else works in balance and no stress or strain occurs.

Horses that come into the yard get settled in and do a little work, then if the rider feels they have a problem they will discuss it with Buffy. Top horses have an MOT once a season, and Maggie checks the horses on a month-by-month basis.

Nutrition

Correct nutrition is vital for the horses' health. All the horses in the yard have their diets monitored.

If a horse is working hard it might need a little extra vitamin E. Horses in hard work should have at least 2000 to 2500 units of vitamin E a day. Bags of feed should state the content per kilo, but as forage does not provide much in the way of vitamin E it is quite possible for a hard-working horse to have a deficiency. Vitamin E helps muscle function and acts as an anti-oxidant, so when the muscles are working hard and are likely to come under attack from free radicals, which cause tissue damage, then the anti-oxidants mop up the free radicals and limit the effect of fatigue on the muscles. As a result the horses' stamina improves, as does their recovery post-exercise; it also helps the immune system. Blood samples showing low-grade muscle damage can indicate a lack of vitamin E, and horses on feeds with high oil content need to be monitored in particular, as the oil increases the demand for vitamin E. This could possibly up the requirement to 3000 units per day or, in the case of a successful racehorse, between 3000 and 5000 units per day.

Selenium, too, is an anti-oxidant and, if supplemented at an appropriate level together with vitamin E, can be very beneficial, especially if the forage has been grown on selenium-poor land or was rained on after cutting so leaching out the minerals.

Good-quality forage is essential as it contains healthy levels of minerals and a good balance of calcium to phosphorus. Magnesium and potassium are also present. Good hay or haylage can make a big difference, as what may appear to be a virus might simply be a lack of protein and minerals. Most of the concentrated feeds are so well formulated now that it is likely most horses receive the trace minerals and vitamins they need, with the possible exception of vitamin E.

It does no harm to give the horses a good supply of forage constantly, unless, of course, they are complete gluttons. This will help maintain an appropriate body balance of minerals and hydration, which is vital for optimal muscle function. Good forage is also important from the respiratory point of view. For some horses that are not good at absorbing calcium and magnesium, alfalfa chaff provides an excellent source of highly absorbable calcium, magnesium and potassium, all of which can also be given in powder form. Peanuts in the height of the competition season might need a little extra calcium and magnesium because he can get nervous and these both help, although he does not have any other problems.

The occasional horse needs a low-salt diet, so the adding of electrolytes to feeds needs to be done with great care as it is possible to push the salt level too high and cause muscle cramps, especially if the compound feed is high in salt. An electrolyte is basically calcium, magnesium, potassium and salt, all of which can be found in a good, appropriate mix used together with good hay and something like Alpha A or its equivalent. Unless a horse has a particular problem, giving electrolytes should not be necessary, not to mention the possibility of tipping the horse over the top. All horses are individual and, if a rider has a concern, a fractional electrolyte test would highlight any problems. This test checks sodium, potassium, calcium, magnesium and phosphorus levels in the blood and urine, and if the sodium levels are too high then it

The yard at Hooze Farm.

suggests that the horse is getting too much salt and would benefit from a lower salt diet.

Young horses in the yard routinely have a blood test every six months, although because we know they receive a good diet and correct training we hope nothing of any significance will show up. If, however, there is an infection or muscle damage, it will be detected at an early stage and treated accordingly.

Buffy supplies all the horses with her own Equitonic, a herbal medicine which helps respiratory problems and minimises viral infections, and all the horses in the yard do very well on it. Donald had a respiratory problem two to three years ago and has to have a little extra care, but the Equitonic helps and on-going maintenance means prevention.

Stabling and ventilation

Good ventilation and clean stables are vital in keeping horses comfortable and free of respiratory problems. Clean, dust-free bedding that has not been in the stable too long (so mould spores have not had a chance to get established) is important, together with a fresh environment. Plenty of air movement, but not draughts, at horse height helps, and we'd prefer to put an extra rug on a horse if it is cold rather than shut a window. There should be no condensation on the walls, and hay should be fed wet and preferably on the ground to give the horse's nasal passages a chance to drain. A low-grade bacterial infection in the lungs will knock any horse down so that it does not thrive and its coat becomes dull.

THE PHYSIOTHERAPIST - Maggie Turner

Maggie is a chartered physiotherapist, having trained for over five years with humans before going on to do further training in order to become qualified to treat horses. Specialising on the back, the method she applies is the Ellis technique in reflex inhibition and soft tissue release. She is further trained in McTimoney chiropractic techniques, which involve treating the whole back from top to tail. Most problems in horses' backs are muscular, with stiffening of the vertebral column within certain areas called 'facet locking'. On the whole, muscles form the bulk of the problems and are mainly due to trauma and accidents (such as being cast); other problems stem from lower down, like leg injuries which result in back pain, which is where Buffy and Maggie work very much together. By law (in Britain), physiotherapists such as Maggie can only work in conjunction with a vet. This is in the best interests of all horses as joint problems can lead to back problems and vice versa, and unless the physio and the vet know what the other is doing, then a problem may not be fully resolved.

Young horses should be checked before they start work. If they have sustained trauma in the field, or while lungeing or loose schooling, it can be identified and tackled straight away. If a horse is given a clean bill of health before the hard work begins, then that is reassuring to know; alternatively, if, for example, a pelvic injury is discovered, then the appropriate amount of rest can be given to the horse to allow it the time to recover and no further trauma sustained.

Maggie checks the horses' backs before and after major competitions, particularly if there is a great deal of travelling involved. She and Buffy will be in contact at least four days a week to discuss problems so that everyone has a clear picture of what is going on.

Peanuts has never really had any muscular skeletal problems as he is not that type. Horses, like human athletes, vary individually but there are some that are always dogged with problems and others that get off very lightly. Peanuts is well balanced and well muscled so seldom has a problem.

Riders, particularly in dressage, can have a detrimental effect on their horses' backs for the following reasons:

- They don't allow sufficient warm-up time. The muscles need to warm up and stretch before more collected work takes place.

- After long periods of collection, the horses are not allowed to swing over their back and relax but are often simply stopped and taken back to their stables.

- They go straight into collected work such as piaffe, passage and pirouettes rather than warming up appropriately and doing these movements some half to threequarters of the way through the training session.

- Often, at the end of a session (when the horse is tired), the last thing a rider does is ask the horse to do extended trot across the diagonal, whereas the task would have been better requested much earlier on. Once completed, instead of winding down, the horse is simply dropped on a long rein and put away.

Common sense dictates that taking care in a training regime and incorporating warming up and cooling down is not only good for the horses psychologically but physically as well.

Finally, another thing that has an important influence on the horse is the rider's own back or hip problems. If a rider is not riding straight (symmetrically) it can immediately influence the horse. Riders must do as much as they can to get themselves right, otherwise the horse has an extra problem to contend with.

THE FARRIER - Simon Gisborne

Simon is in charge of all matters concerning the feet. Like Maggie, he too works closely with Buffy, since so many lamenesses stem from foot problems.

Following a four-year apprenticeship, Simon has spent over seventeen years shoeing horses in a variety of yards. Not a person to follow fashion, Simon shoes each horse according to its individual needs and his opinion is immediately sought if a problem occurs.

The input from a farrier is vital to the performance of any top competition horse. Too often, a farrier is judged by the length of time a shoe stays on for, when in fact, if a horse is shod with the length and width of the foot in mind, usually it should be shod more frequently. A horse is shod for conformation and performance and according to its needs, thus ensuring minimal disruption to the horse's natural balance.

Shoeing trends are a difficult area, with some owners trying to keep up with the latest fashions. Glue-on shoes, for example, can be expensive and should only be used when appropriate in cases of remedial work. For Simon the most important thing is to shoe appropriately. Usually my horses are shod every five to six weeks and, on the whole, because all the horses have such a good diet, there are very few problems. The horses that do have a few problems are the two really big horses, Hector and Donald.

Hector is very pigeon-toed with very flat feet. Egg-bar shoes at the back give him extra support because he is low on his heels. He has slightly odd feet too, so egg-bars give the maximum support. Because of the shape of these shoes they add 25 per cent more ground-bearing surface to the foot,

Farrier Simon, with Santas.

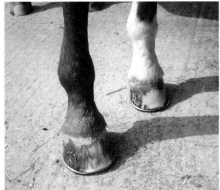

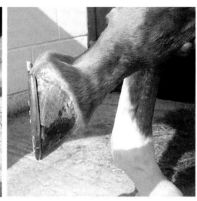

Donald's two front feet and the shoes that he wears. The left foot is a size bigger than the right; notice how the right one is smaller and more upright. Simon makes sure that Donald's front shoes have plenty of length.

and because the extra ground-bearing surface is concentrated around the heels, it gives greater support to the heel area. Egg-bars should be used where there is an abnormal force bearing down on the heels, such as in horses with long, sloping pasterns.

Donald also has difficult feet. His front feet are two different sizes, one being size 7 the other being size 8. From the front they are two completely different feet, with one being very flat and the other very small and upright. Each foot has to be shod individually, and as a rule he will be shod every four to five weeks.

Santas has good feet which are even all the way round. The only criticism would be that they are quite long in the toe behind. With the length of toe and the fact that he is low on the heel, he is shod long to give length. He is shod in 'Natural Balance' shoes, which seem to suit him. They help horses with flat feet because they place the breakover point much further back, and horses often work much better in them (and stumble less) as a result. Natural Balance shoes are much wider than conventional shoes, with a square toe.

Horses with very long, flat front feet are not helped by having clips on the very front of their shoes and this again is where Natural Balance shoes help, as the farrier can shorten up the toe and shoe long at the heel, and the extra length means that the horse can get a better angle through the leg. If the horse

The Natural Balance shoe.

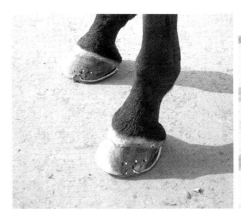 

Long shoeing, lengthening the heels.

is not shod with this length then he would be even lower on his heels, so weakening the horse in this area. If a foot is upright, then the angle is too upright, and the farrier has to lower the heel slightly by shoeing with plenty of length.

When dressage horses are working to the maximum with their hindquarters lowered and their hind legs engaged, the strain on the lower hind legs is greatly increased. Without the correct shoeing, some of these horses might well break down. However, if they are shod long, which stops them dropping right down, then they are at far less risk. This is why egg-bars are quite often seen on dressage horses. It is best, though, to try to correct the foot through lengthening first before resorting to egg-bars.

The bottom line is all about getting your horses' diets right and then having your horses' feet done regularly and appropriately, and doing what is best for your horses. By doing exactly what Simon instructs us to do, I find my horses have very few problems.

Groom Caroline Dawson, with Peanuts, awaiting the prize-giving.

Good Luck!

The whole art of a successful career at the top is down to team effort, which I hope I have made apparent throughout this book.

Before signing off, I would like to stress the importance of listening to and enjoying your horses, for it is this that makes dressage, and riding generally, fascinating and pleasurable. Horses that are given time and patience **can** develop into stars.

Remember to have fun along the way – I certainly have!

CARL HESTER

Index

Page numbers in **bold** type refer to illustrations